Find A Balance. Fuel

EAT LIKE A CHAMP
Basic Healthy Eating Habits for the Everyday Athlete
by Reni Towns

OVER 30 HEALTHY RECIPES

Copyright © 2015 Reni Towns
All rights reserved.
No portion of this book may be reproduced mechanically, electronically, or by any other means, including photocopying, without written permission of the author or publisher. It is illegal to copy this book, post it to a website, or distribute it by any other means without permission from the author or publisher.

ISBN: 0986135909
ISBN-13: 978-0986135903 (Reni Towns - Health Coach)

Limits of Liability and Disclaimer of Warranty

The author and publisher shall not be liable for your misuse of this material. This book is strictly for informational and educational purposes.

Warning—Disclaimer

The purpose of this book is to educate and entertain. The author and/or publisher do not guarantee that anyone following these techniques, suggestions, tips, ideas, or strategies will become successful. The author and/or publisher shall have neither liability nor responsibility to anyone with respect to any loss or damage caused, or alleged to be caused, directly or indirectly by the information contained in this book.

DEDICATION

This book is dedicated to all the Everyday Athletes who work hard to be healthy.

TABLE OF CONTENTS

Dedication iii
Table of Contents v
Acknowledgments vii
Who is the Everyday Athlete? 1
The Food and Fitness Connection 5
Core Nutrition Concepts 15
    Mindfulness 16
    Bio-Individuality 18
    Crowding Out 21
    Real Food 23

Eat Like A Champ 27
    Sugar 27
    Fruits and Veggies 29
    Protein 33
    Healthy Fats 35
    Water 37

The Nutrition Game Plan 43
    Planning 43
    Accountability 47
    Tracking 50
    Measuring Success 53

The Eat Like a Champ Playbook............55
Recipes 59
    Breakfast 59
    Lunch 68
    Snacks 76
    Dinner 82
Daily Food and Fitness Journal............99
Works Cited 121
About the Author 124

ACKNOWLEDGMENTS

THANK YOU TO EVERYONE who has been supportive of my journey to health and happiness!

I would especially like to thank my Mom and Dad, from packing my lunches to shooting hoops in the driveway and introducing me to organic food, thank you for helping me build a healthy foundation.

Thanks also go to my favorite retired athletes, Lucie and Buddy, for insisting I enjoy several walks a day and encouraging me to relax and partake in an afternoon nap once in a while.

Finally, a special thank you to Matt for carrying heavy bags of produce home from the farmers market, sampling new recipes and cheering me on as I crossed the finish line at too many races to count.

1
WHO IS THE EVERYDAY ATHLETE?

THERE ARE A LOT of interesting books written by or about incredible athletes: the NBA basketball player who stepped up his game with weight-lifting, the ultra-marathon runner who beat cancer, the Olympian who trained for hours to win gold. Those stories are inspiring, but this book is a different type of nutrition book. This book is for the athlete who has a full-time job and family responsibilities. This is for the athlete who works out for fun and stress relief. This is for the athlete who feels better when they are exercising regularly but sometimes struggle to fit it in with a busy schedule. This book is for the Everyday Athlete. Many Everyday Athletes grew up playing sports and being active. Some adopted fitness later in life and worked hard to make it part of their daily routine. They enjoy competition, working up a sweat, and they appreciate the physical skills that result from a regular fitness routine. But as the Everyday Athlete matures, sometimes their regularly planned workouts might not be enough. They get tired. They gain weight. They lose interest in the gym. Are **YOU** an Everyday Athlete?

I consider myself an Everyday Athlete. I grew up playing basketball, soccer and volleyball in school. My parents were always schlepping me from practice or to a game. I spent hours on the weekends in my driveway shooting hoops and spent summers at various sports camps. Athletics have always been a part of my life and as an adult I still find ways to maintain an exercise schedule because I feel better when I'm staying active. I enjoy fitness, but I also have a lot of other things going on. I enjoy working out, but I don't have time to spend hours in the gym. I need quick and efficient workouts that I can balance with a busy schedule.

This book is intended to reignite the spark for the Everyday Athlete through disclosing the critical relationship between food and fitness. Instead of using exercise as a solution to poor eating habits, good nutrition should be considered a critical piece of the puzzle along with fitness to help improve the overall health and wellness of the Everyday Athlete. This book will teach you how to Eat Like A Champ.

Eating Like A Champ is not about counting calories and restrictive low-fat diets. It's not about a specific food product or dietary theory. It's not necessarily about weight-loss, although that might be a happy benefit. Eating Like A Champ is about enjoying great- tasting and nutritious food. It's about well-balanced, guilt-free meal plans. It's about finding the right foods for your body to help you hit your fitness goals as an Everyday Athlete. Eating Like A Champ empowers Everyday Athletes to develop healthy food and fitness habits so they can look and feel their best.

In order to Eat Like A Champ, you need to make your health a priority. You may already be doing a lot of things right, such as maintaining a regular fitness routine. If not, maybe you want to take the steps to do so. If you are looking for a specific list of food you should or shouldn't eat, you won't get that here (although you will find some delicious recipes to try towards the back of this book). Instead, this book will support you as you take ownership to discover what works for you using some general guidelines and resources for planning and tracking. Eating Like A Champ will help you develop healthy food and fitness habits. By recognizing the need to eat healthy to improve your health, you are taking the first step to Eating Like A Champ. If you are starting a new fitness habit or looking to overhaul your nutrition, you may want to consult a health professional first to ensure you are starting off on the right foot.

It may be difficult at first. These new foods may not taste great at first. It may take time to learn how to cook, and there may be a few spectacular kitchen failures along the way. It may take a few attempts before you find the right recipes to create healthy meal plans. Some of the processed foods you may have been eating in the past can actually impact your taste buds; processed foods loaded with sugar, salt and oil can actually numb your taste buds and impact the way whole foods will taste to you (Krishan). It may take some time to cleanse your system. You may need to try new, healthy foods several times, prepared in different way to learn what you like. It can take Everyday Athletes some time to identify a favorite workout to help motivate them to exercise regularly, and it can also take some time to discover the healthy foods that taste great. Be patient. Try a lot of different kinds of foods. Listen to your body. Stick with it. You WILL be rewarded. Eating Like A Champ helps Everyday Athletes feel their best.

2
THE FOOD AND FITNESS CONNECTION

Since I grew up playing team sports, I had many amazing coaches who taught me many life lessons that have impacted me both on and off the field. I *learned* the mechanics of a turnaround jump shot in basketball. I *learned* concepts of leadership as captain of my college soccer team. I *learned* how to dive with proper form to avoid injuries in volleyball. I *learned* the importance of teamwork. I *learned* how to strength-train in the off-season. I *learned* how to "get back on the horse" after a tough loss. But one thing I **never learned** about in my days as a student athlete was the importance of nutrition. In fact, most of my direct associations with food and sports were about fast food, like celebrating a big wins with pizza or ice cream after the game.

Most days, my Mom worked hard to provide balanced meals. We ate dinners with some protein, carbohydrates and vegetables. My lunches were packed in a brown paper bag with a turkey sandwich, an apple, with a couple cookies for dessert. When I was younger I didn't pay attention to my eating habits; I wish I knew then what I know now. Ideally, we would develop healthy eating habits as kids. We would love kale and quinoa and we would opt to eat broccoli instead of cookies. Swapping broccoli for cookies might be a stretch, but some kids are eating all kinds of fruits and vegetables. But for those of us who didn't grow up with produce from the local farmers market or the backyard garden we need to learn how to love healthy food as adults. This can be difficult – breaking old habits and making new ones requires dedication.

Growing up, I didn't think too much about what I was eating, but when I went away to college and had to fend for myself, I simply didn't eat balanced meals. Sugar cereals, diet soda, and late night pizza – I ate junk food. I was lucky to have the opportunity to play on the women's soccer team, so I stayed very physically active. While I managed to avoid the dreaded "Freshman 15", I did gain around 7.5 pounds thanks to my poor eating habits.

Fast forward to after college… I moved to Chicago, and got a respectable job in corporate America. My days of daily (sometimes twice daily) workouts came to a halt. I drove over an hour to commute to the suburbs each way, every day. I worked from 8-ish in the morning to 5-ish at night (sometimes later). I sat at a desk, in a cubicle, in front of a computer all day. As a young adult, I didn't know how to cook, so I usually went out to eat or stayed in and ate microwave dinners. I was getting up early, guzzling multiple Starbucks to stay awake, and eating mostly takeout or restaurant food. Luckily, I inherited a few healthy habits from my family and still ate a few vegetables, but that wasn't enough. I was tired. I felt lethargic, and I was gaining weight. Sound familiar? I knew something had to change. So I went back to what I knew: exercise.

I joined a gym and a few adult sports teams, and made an effort to try to do something physically active every day. I started running for fun – a concept I once thought was crazy if it didn't involve chasing after a ball or an opponent – and I even signed up for a few 5Ks. I lost a little bit of the weight I had gained, but I was still very lethargic and noticed I wasn't always "giving it my all" during my workouts, especially after a long day. I was still eating poorly: burgers, fries, diet soda. I figured I just needed to work out more and work out harder. So I signed up for a half marathon.

Long distance runners are all skinny, right?

Admittedly, I was very nervous to train and run a half marathon. I barely had enough courage to call myself a "real runner". I joined a charity running team for some extra support and motivation. In doing so, I helped the group raise money for breast cancer research, and they helped me by providing a training plan and motivation. I was running more than ever – and I was **HUNGRY!** So I ate. I ate a lot. And I ate without real consideration for what I was eating. *Chicago-style deep-dish pizza? Yes, please! I'll have an extra slice because I'm training for a half marathon and I ran 6 miles today! I ran 8 miles today so I deserve a pint of Ben and Jerry's ice cream.* You get the picture.

Overall, my first half marathon was an amazing experience. I felt a huge sense of accomplishment at the end for having raised money for charity, for sticking with my training plan, and for crossing that finish line on race day. The downer: I had actually gained weight while training for my big race. Cut to the light bulb going on over my head…

Fitness alone, even strenuous training, is not enough to maintain a healthy weight and lifestyle. The food you put into your mouth is fuel for your body. I realized I needed to stop eating junk food and the like, and start paying attention to my nutrition. Using women's fitness magazines as my primary resources, I started my journey of healthy eating…. Or so I thought.

Most of what I read focused on caloric intake and output: eat less, work out more. I started tracking all the food I ate and counting calories. It was harder to track calories in restaurant food, but I didn't know how to cook. I started grocery shopping more frequently, buying low-fat, low-calorie processed foods so I knew exactly how many calories I was taking in. I was eating a lot of microwave dinners with packaging that touted "healthy" and "lean" food. I also suspected organic food was important, so I started shopping more at the fancy health food store. I made sure to pick out boxes of food that were labeled as "organic." I was very impressed with their salad bar and produce options, so I started eating more salads. I was sticking to my calorie goals. I was working out regularly, and I finally began to lose some weight. But as I trained for my next race, I started experiencing stomach pains and cramping during my long training runs. There were several times when I was literally running to find a bathroom during my run! While some consider this to be some sort of rite of passage for distance runners, it caused me anxiety and stress. On top of this, I was often exhausted, and I felt hungry all the time. I found counting calories was really time-consuming and annoying! I had a series of very disappointing races where I had to slow down and/or walk because of my physical digestive discomfort. While I had lost some weight, I still wasn't feeling good and knew I needed to continue to make some changes.

During this time, a lot happened in my personal life. I met and married my husband. We started cooking together at home more often. We rescued a retired racing Greyhound named Lucie who needed daily walks since our living space did not include a backyard. And after some discussion, we packed up a few things and moved across the country to Portland, Oregon.

Moving to the Pacific Northwest was a big change. When we first arrived in Portland, My husband was job-hunting and we worked to stay on a strict budget, which meant no restaurant dinners and more cooking at home. I discovered we could save money by shopping locally at the wonderful farmers markets throughout the city. By having easy access to amazingly fresh produce and artisan goods, we were motivated to cook more. I was shocked by how relaxed and comfortable I was getting in my kitchen. I didn't even need to follow recipes most nights. As I became more comfortable, I stopped relying on packaged, processed foods. It also helped that Chicago-style deep-dish pizza was no longer an easily available option. I started to notice improvements in my mood and energy levels. Oh, and I dropped a few pounds too.

I became more interested in nutrition and cooking and started to consider the possibility of pursuing this line of work as a career. I suspected there was more to nutrition than what I was absorbing in my fitness magazines, and some of the cooking magazines I had started reading focused on complicated recipes that didn't seem very healthy. Through additional research and soul searching, I eventually ended up completing a health coach training program through the Institute for Integrative Nutrition˚. I received training on hundreds of dietary theories and nutrition concepts, and I learned how to apply them for others and myself. Basically, I discovered how to eat healthy and how to help others live a healthy life. I no longer need to count calories. I feel energized. I now know how to listen to my body and make adjustments as my workouts change. In short, I learned how to Eat Like A Champ.

It took me a while to get here, but it was worth it. In my work as a Health Coach, I want to prevent people from struggling like I did. I want to help cut to the chase and share my healthy food and fitness habits. I want to partner with busy people, the Everyday Athletes, who enjoy staying active and help them to manage stress or establish fitness routines. Everyday Athletes have a lot on their plates: full-time jobs and/or family responsibilities, as well as social commitments. They work hard to squeeze in their exercise routines most days. They may need some support to balance their fitness routine with healthy eating habits. I am here to ensure that Everyday Athletes can develop lasting habits to incorporate healthy eating alongside their fitness routine for optimal wellness.

I always thought that staying physically active was the most important component of a healthy lifestyle. I was only half right. Learning to cook and Eat Like A Champ has done just as much or even more for my health than running a half marathon on its own did.

Once I realized I had to change my eating habits, it took me a while to get my bearings. I knew I needed to stop eating out so much and the microwave dinners were not cutting it. I wanted to start cooking, but I had no idea where to start.

As I mentioned, my mom ensured we grew up with balanced meals, but she wasn't a chef and didn't particularly like cooking. We ate a lot of plain, baked chicken seasoned with salt and pepper alongside white rice and green beans. I didn't have any impression that cooking could be simple and fun. But even though my mom didn't teach me how to cook, she did get me started on the path of gaining interest in nutrition. After she was diagnosed with breast cancer, she started to make some changes to her and my dad's diet. She started buying organic food. She made sure her milk and other dairy products were hormone-free. She sought out humanely raised animal protein. Although I had already moved out of the house, I took notice of the changes my mom was making, and I started to try to incorporate her new habits into my own diet.

I began to buy healthier foods, but I still needed to figure out the cooking thing. I needed something simple as I was still working long hours, commuting, and trying to work out. I started by making pasta because it was easy and fast. I switched to whole-wheat pasta. I bought a small food processor and started making my own sauce and added lots of extra veggies into it. Salads became a part of my everyday routine. These small changes helped, but it seemed I still had so much to learn. I was getting pretty tired of eating pasta every day.

I started watching the Food Network. It was very intimidating. Those chefs made it look easy, but I couldn't dice vegetables like that. I saw commercials for Rachael Ray's 30-Minute Meals – that sounded like my speed, so I TiVo'd a bunch of episodes and would watch a series of them on weekends for inspiration. I even asked Santa for some Rachael Ray cookbooks for Christmas, and I started cooking by following her recipes. Her 30-Minute Meals took me longer than 30 minutes – they often had long lists of ingredients and spices I didn't have, but I'd try a new recipe every weekend. I was single at the time, so I always had leftovers that I could eat during the week. Slowly but surely, I started to learn what flavors worked well and which ingredient combinations were tasty. I looked for ways to modify the recipes I found – either by adding in more veggies or by simplifying some of the ingredient lists.

By the time I met my husband, I was cooking more, but I was nowhere near a Top Chef. For one of our first dates, he offered to cook dinner, which was one of the first signs that he was a keeper. He knew I shopped at the local Whole Foods and tried to eat organic whenever possible, so he took his first trip to the "healthy" grocery store to prep for our date and get ingredients. He later told me that he was shocked by how expensive it was and had hoped I was worth it – ha! After years of marriage and healthy eating (that he now appreciates most of the time), I'd say it was well worth it. I was pleasantly surprised that the recipe he had chosen for our first time cooking together was a Rachael Ray chicken piccata pasta toss dish. It was very tasty and we had fun cooking together that first time, and I'm happy to say that was the first of many. We enjoy cooking together to this day and I'm very lucky he has been encouraging and supportive of my interest in nutrition.

It took time for me to gain confidence in the kitchen. I needed to be proactive, and I needed to invest in some cooking gadgets. It helps to have a partner to cook with and to offer support. There have been some botched cooking experiments, but that is OK – it makes the successful endeavors that much more delicious. While I still don't consider myself a great chef, I have gained confidence in the kitchen. I had no formal training and lack many skills that the true culinary experts have, but through trial and error, I have learned what works and what tastes good. I have a few go-to dishes for every season and I love exploring new recipes and seeking inspiration to create to meals. I even learned to appreciate a vast array of spices beyond salt and pepper!

I think the backbone to cooking at home is selecting quality ingredients that are good for you. Understanding a few different cooking techniques is also helpful, and knowing how to use a few gadgets doesn't hurt. Most importantly, it is crucial to have fun in the kitchen. Cooking should not feel like a chore. Instead, it is your opportunity to create healthy fuel for yourself and your family, to help provide you with the energy to enjoy life. It is also a way to fuel your workouts and help sustain you as an Everyday Athlete for years.

Learning how to fuel your workouts is a lot like learning to cook: lots of trial and error, lots of practice. I had some failed attempts, and some amazing successes. As you develop your cooking skills, you will notice which food works well before a tough workout, and which food does not. By using quality ingredients, you will begin to notice a difference in your energy levels and performance. As a side benefit, you may even drop a few pounds.

As you start cooking using quality ingredients, you are starting to Eat Like A Champ. Cooking does NOT have to be complicated. It can be very simple. I often seek to create very simple meals, using only 2-4 ingredients. I consider the ingredients I like, and think about a well-balanced meal, sometimes simply picking a vegetable, a protein and a whole grain. I might add a spice, but often stick to my roots with good old salt and pepper. The method of cooking could vary by time of year – roasting in the winter or grilling in the summer, for example. I might also take one of my favorite recipes and swap one of the ingredients with something new. Or I might work to create something based on what I have sitting in the fridge. Inspiration comes in many forms and I rarely follow a recipe these days, unless I'm trying something new.

The fact that my food choices were impacting my energy level never occurred to me. I would try to get more sleep and when that failed I'd try to compensate with more coffee. For a while at work, I had the nickname "Caramel Macchiato" because of my frequent visits to the coffee cart throughout the day. The caffeine and sugar boost would help in the short term, but in the long term it actually contributed more to my lack of energy.

Working out generally helped increase my energy level, although it was difficult to get motivated some days. The first 10 minutes of my workout were typically pretty painful, but once I got going, I felt better. I made working out a priority, and, as a result, I would often feel an endorphin rush during and after my workouts. However, I was not fueling properly for the workouts, and wasn't truly getting the most out of them. I needed something to feel balanced throughout the day. I wanted to have energy going into a workout so I could push myself harder. Instead of relying on the endorphin rush after a workout, I wanted to feel energized going into a workout.

The Everyday Athlete needs to consider both food and fitness into their health and wellness program. By putting the same, or more, effort into meal planning through cooking at home and making healthy food choices as you put into your fitness routine, you will reap the benefits of Eating Like A Champ.

3
CORE NUTRITION CONCEPTS

IF YOU ARE READING this book, you are likely an Everyday Athlete. You may have a regular fitness routine or you are working to develop one, and now you want to know exactly what to eat and when. There are many books written by amazing athletes and their tried and true nutrition plans that they swear by. When I first realized I needed to change my eating habits, I tried to find the right book to help me, and actually become frustrated with my options. While it is inspiring to hear how an incredible athlete thrived on a specific diet, I would often feel like a failure when their plan didn't work for me.

I am not an elite athlete and I don't have the resources of one, such as a trainer or a personal chef. When I was seeking nutrition advice, I needed some down-to-earth guidance that would be easy to implement on my own based on my unique situation and schedule. Through my studies at the Institute of Integrative Nutrition® and beyond, I have identified several core nutrition concepts to provide this framework so other Everyday Athletes can Eat Like A Champ: **1) Mindfulness, 2) Bio-Individuality, 3) Crowding Out, and 4) Real Food**. Each of these will be explained in detail.

Mindfulness

Mindfulness means being aware of something and focusing on the sensations of the present moment. Applying this concept to eating took me a while to adopt, and I still need to work hard to retain mindfulness when it comes to my nutrition. It is too easy for me to start eating mindlessly when I get stressed and busy. Before I made the connection between food and fitness, and before I adopted the core nutrition concepts, even when I tried to eat healthy, without mindfulness, I was not able to truly appreciate how I was fueling my fitness. As you begin to be more mindful with your nutrition, you can begin to leverage strategies such as crowding out and selecting real food, which will be discussed in a future chapter.

It is so easy to go into autopilot mode when you get busy. In some ways, being on autopilot makes it easier to execute an Everyday Athlete's fitness plan when you are feeling tired and run-down. Back in the day, I would often go into a zombie-like state when I went to the gym to crank out 30 minutes on the treadmill or elliptical. I'm sure you've seen some "fitness zombies" in the gym. When I succumbed to this state, mindless eating after a workout seemed to be a likely outcome. This mindlessness may stem from our good intentions to finish a daily workout without feeling energized. To snap out of it, you need to increase your energy, which will come by Eating Like A Champ. One way to do this is to become more mindful of your nutrition. The core nutrition concepts discussed in this book will help you develop a mindset for mindful eating. This mindset consists of breathing, adjusting portion-size and slowing down your eating.

One way to start eating more mindfully is to stop and take a few deep breaths before eating anything. Consider how you are feeling. Are you truly hungry, or are you stressed or bored? Are you eating simply because its noon and you are supposed to eat lunch? It is so easy to get caught up in our busy schedules and eating on the run, we don't even stop and think about what or how much we are eating every day.

As you take those few deep breaths, make sure you step away from your task at hand. With mobile devices and Wi-Fi everywhere, we are constantly consuming digital content, making it that much easier to consume food mindlessly. Stopping to breathe and stepping away from your screens mid-meal can also help your mindful eating.

Next, consider portion size. I grew up with a rule around finishing my dinner – I couldn't leave the table to play outside or watch TV until I finished my dinner. Since my mom cooked mostly healthy, well-balanced meals, this rule was to urge my brother and me not to waste food and discourage us from being picky. This probably led to my sense of adventure when it comes to food – I'll try anything at least once – but this habit hasn't always served me well as an adult going out to eat and cleaning my plate with rich, oversized restaurant portions. Even when cooking at home, it can be easy to supersize a portion of my favorite dishes. I try to make it a habit to divide my restaurant portions in half to be more mindful. I also work to pause midway through to check-in with my hunger both at restaurants and at home. It's not uncommon for our eyes to be bigger than our stomachs, so making an effort to pause, think and breathe during meals is another way to exercise mindful eating practices.

Slow down! I am often reminded of this next mindfulness application as I'm feeding my dogs. My pups are very food-motivated and they get very excited to eat. As soon as we put their food down, they attack their food bowls, often not even taking the time to chew their food. It's not uncommon for them to gulp down their food within 5 minutes and then spend 20 minutes prowling around the kitchen looking for more food because they think they are still hungry. There are times when I find myself scarfing down my meals as well, taking big bites and not chewing very thoroughly.

In my efforts to eat mindfully, breathing and taking a moment before and during my meals, I also make it a point to remind myself to take smaller bites and really chew my food. I aim to chew each bite 20-30 times. There are some schools of nutrition, such as macrobiotics, that suggest people chew each mouthful of food 50 times or more (Kushi Institute). The process of digestion starts in your mouth and the more you chew your food, the easier it is for your digestive system to do its job. By taking smaller bites and chewing more thoroughly, you can also help your body feel fuller and possibly reduce how much food you are consuming. You'll also be less likely to go back to the kitchen to prowl for more food when you are done!

By taking a mindful approach to your nutrition, you become aware of how it impacts your body and your energy levels. You will begin to notice how your food fuels your fitness programs. This will help you acknowledge the critical link between food and fitness so you can Eat Like A Champ.

As an Everyday Athlete, you can also be mindful with your workout plans. This includes listening to your body when you are injured and/or need a recovery day. It is not uncommon for Everyday Athletes to push themselves too hard, so adopting a mindfulness practice in various aspects of your wellness can have many benefits.

Bio-Individuality

Everyday Athletes are busy people. As a result, I often work with busy clients who want me to give them a shortcut and tell them exactly what to eat. They ask what I eat and if they can just follow my personal plan. It isn't always that simple. What works well for me, might not work for you. This book isn't the "silver bullet" of nutrition plans that will work for all Everyday Athletes, but it will give you, as a unique individual, an understanding of nutrition basics and some tools to use so you can Eat Like A Champ.

Embracing the core concept of bio-individuality has helped me let go of a lot of wellness "baggage". The concept of bio-individuality means that there is no "one size fits all" nutrition plan; each person is unique with very specific nutrition requirements (Rosenthal 35). When I first started my health and wellness journey, I read a lot of books and magazine articles about specific nutrition theories. When I didn't have any luck with them, I'd think I was doing something wrong or maybe that there was something wrong with me. As an avid animal lover and proud "parent" of two rescue dogs, there was a strong part of me drawn to the ideals of a vegetarian diet. However, when I tried to follow it strictly, I'd feel lethargic. After hearing of so many successful athletes who had great success with the Paleo Diet, I tried it and found it wasn't a great fit either.

There were aspects of each that I found helpful. Through studying a lot of different nutrition concepts, I was able to try a variety of meal plans and learned what worked well and what didn't. I gave myself permission not to feel guilty about eating some animal protein and found comfort in eating whole grains from time to time. But I learned to limit animal protein, select quality-sourced food, and incorporate nuts and seeds. **And that is what bio-individuality is all about – finding what works best for you.**

Finding your bio-individual nutrition plan requires an open mind and patience. It's important not to compare yourself to others, whether it's an elite athlete or another Everyday Athlete. It is also important not to project your nutrition plan onto others. What works for one Everyday Athlete might not work for another.

By adopting an attitude of mindfulness and using some of the techniques in this book, you will learn to build your unique nutrition plan so you can Eat Like A Champ.

Getting started may feel overwhelming. You might be following certain wellness practices because you think they are healthy or you know they've worked for someone else. Instead of forcing a square peg into a round hole, move on to a new concept that helps you achieve your goals. There are hundreds of nutrition theories and many of them provide conflicting approaches. Investing in some professional guidance and support can make a big difference. A Health Coach can help you navigate through the information and develop a unique plan with additional support.

There are many factors that can influence Everyday Athlete's bio-individuality, including age, ancestry, geography, and gender just to name a few. It is feasible that your nutrition needs may change each season, as you age, or if you move to a new area. Therefore, you will want to remain open-minded and mindful, especially during periods of transition and stress, so you can adjust your nutrition plan as needed. You may find, for example, in a period of healing or recovery, you may require a strict elimination diet to help identify any food sensitivities that may be causing inflammation or other health concerns. At different times in your life you might be able to introduce certain foods back into your meal planning. During specific seasons or training cycles, you may require more animal protein or carbohydrates. There may be other foods you will learn you consistently need to avoid in order to feel your best.

As you begin to Eat Like A Champ, work to start with a clean slate and let go of any preconceived notions regarding nutrition. It can be helpful to consider varying approaches and take away kernels of each theory that resonate with you and generate the results you are looking for. Be aware of when it is time to adjust and make changes, and be open to the adjustments.

Crowding Out

Many diets have very specific rules about what you cannot eat. They focus on what you need to stop eating effective immediately. Many diets are all about restrictions. For example, don't eat cookies and ice cream, or don't exceed 1,200 calories a day. This typically makes me want to eat that forbidden food even more! I used to work very hard to stick to my calorie target and not eat any treats, and I could usually pull it off Monday through Thursday.

Once the weekend came, the cravings would hit me. I'd rationalize my cravings, thinking about how good I did all week and that I could go for an extra-long run sometime over the weekend. Then, I'd finish a box of cookies. After that, I'd feel disappointed and I'd usually have a stomachache. The long run really didn't sound fun at that point, but I'd force myself to get out there and push through it for a pretty uncomfortable workout. This might lead to making more bad food choices during the weekend and trying to start over on Monday with a very restrictive diet - the vicious cycle would continue.

As I started to learn more about nutrition basics, I realized my approach wasn't setting me up for success. So many people approach nutrition trying so hard not to eat this and that, and they wind up not eating enough, feeling unsatisfied, veering off track, and feeling guilty. Many Everyday Athletes end up not fueling properly, and therefore do not get the best workout. I knew I needed to break this cycle.

When starting to Eat Like A Champ, don't think about what you can't eat anymore. Instead, consider all the wonderfully healthy foods you will to incorporate into your diet. The concept of crowding out suggests you add to your diet instead of taking away (Institute for Integrative Nutrition'). Focus on what you can have and all the benefits that come along with it. By adding in more of the good stuff, you will naturally start to crowd out the junk that is keeping you from your optimal wellness.

The subtle psychological shift that crowding out provides helped me proactively seek out healthier food and feel good about the positive changes that I was making. When I had a treat, it was easier to move on by staying focused on adding in more good options in the future. Since my goal wasn't to stop eating sweets, I wasn't disappointed when I would have one. My goal was to eat more than 5 servings of vegetables, and that was something I could stay focused on each day. **By actively working toward having 2 servings of fruits or vegetables with every meal, I was incorporating more nutrient dense food and I was filling up on real food.** There were simply fewer opportunities for me to eat processed foods or dessert after eating a big bowl of vegetables because I was full. I began to notice changes, including a higher energy level. During the times when I wasn't as energetic, I would consider how many fruits and veggies I was having and I would realize that I might have fallen short of my goals. That would prompt me to focus on crowding out again.

The crowding out technique can be used to eat more vegetables. It can also be used to drink more water. Many Everyday Athletes drink a lot of empty calories – from soda to energy drinks. Crowd out those empty calories by having a glass of water before reaching for a bottle of pop. Start the day with a glass of water before your coffee. Instead of an energy drink as an afternoon pick-me-up, fill up on water. Slowly but surely you will increase your water in-take and you will have less room for the empty calories. **Since staying hydrated is important for an Everyday Athlete, this technique will help your workouts and overall wellness.**

The subtle changes provided a slow transition into very sustainable healthy habits. The change was gradual, and while I was going through it I didn't even realize it was happening, but after a few months, I was consistently eating more vegetable and drinking more water.

Real Food

Have you ever read the labels on processed foods, those that come in boxes? I admit I used to only look at the calorie count. But not all calories are created equal! Packaged foods often contain added sugar and often the ingredients list is often full of things that I can barely pronounce. Processed foods travel long distances to sit on grocery store shelves for long periods of time and then possibly sit in your pantry for even longer periods of time.

A core concept of Eating Like A Champ **is to eat real food, not processed food**. It may not be realistic to eliminate all packaged food from your diet, but you can work to crowd out some specific items and make smarter choices with the packaged goods you purchase.

One significant way you can educate yourself is to read ingredient labels. I used to focus on calories and/or fat content; that is what I thought was important as part of the Standard American Diet (SAD). Since I've learned to Eat Like A Champ, I know not all calories are created equally and some healthy fats are good for me. Now when I look at labels, I focus more on ingredients. First and foremost, do I recognize the ingredients? Can I pronounce them? If not, do I want to be eating this? No! I also check the sugar content. Processed foods often use some form of added sugar, and I aim to limit that. We will discuss sugar specifically in a later section.

Another way to make informed food choices is to select those with packaging that contain fewer toxins and chemicals. For example, I look for canned foods that are BPA-free. According to the Mayo Clinic, BPA (the chemical bisphenol A) can impact brain development and cause behavior problems in children and can possibly cause cancer in adults (Zeratsky). BPA can also be found in plastic containers, so I look to use BPA-free plastics as well. In most cases, goods found in boxes or in glass are great for kitchen use because they are safer materials and you can easily reuse them for items that you buy in bulk.

While ingredients and packaging are two factors to consider when buying packaged food, one that you should not let sway your decision-making is advertising. There is a lot of misleading information in food advertising, and some of it is just plain incorrect. Food advertising is used by organizations to get you to buy their product, not necessarily to promote good health, even if they sometimes try to market the product's healthiness to get you to buy it. In many cases, when foods are labeled as healthy, that usually means the company selling it wants you to think it's healthy so they can have a healthy bottom line.

Big food businesses spend billions of dollars every year on marketing so they can turn a profit. While there may be companies that are truly dedicated to producing healthy products, most large corporations are in business to make money. Most real food doesn't have multi-million dollar ad campaigns. Have you ever seen a commercial for broccoli? Most small organic farmers are focused on growing quality food, even if it is in smaller yields than larger commercial farms. They don't have the budget or resources to create funny commercials starring famous people with catchy theme songs. So I tend to purchase foods that I don't see commercials promoting the product.

Some companies will also try to use the concept of "healthy" in their advertising. Beware of these tactics and understand food labels and certifications. For example, if a product is "all natural" or "heart healthy"-- that really doesn't mean anything. There is a certification process for food products to be labeled USDA Organic so the green and white symbol means the product meets specific standards, which can vary by the type of product. For example, organic produce must be free from irradiation, sewage sludge, synthetic fertilizers, prohibited pesticides, and genetically modified organisms per the United States Department of Agriculture (USDA). One of the best methods of finding healthy products is to read ingredients labels and check sugar and sodium levels. An even better method is to buy fresh food. While fresh produce and animal protein don't last as long as packaged and processed foods, they have the most nutritional benefits and are a great way to crowd out potentially harmful additives and toxins.

There are many food products, such as energy drinks and protein bars, marketed to Everyday Athletes. We need to be cautious with these as well. In many cases, real food is a better option. Let's face it, the bright blue sports drinks and neon pink gels aren't found in nature! As we begin down the road to Eat Like A Champ, keep these concepts in mind and start applying them to your daily routine, as they will help you gradually develops sustainable healthy habits.

My favorite source for real food is my local farmers market. The food that I find there is likely only a few days old and I can taste the difference. I can talk to the farmers about their farming practices and methods and gain their insight into what I'm putting into my body. I eat seasonally grown foods based on what is available and I have fun trying new recipes with new ingredients. My money is going directly to farmers so they can continue to grow, rather than to large companies so they can make more flashy commercials. Joining a local food CSA (community supported agriculture) is another good way to buy seasonally fresh produce from local farmers. It often exposes you to new and different foods (like kohlrabi) that would often be overlooked. To find a local CSA in your area, visit the Local Harvest website: www.localharvest.org/csa. I feel good about supporting local agricultural and feel confident about the quality of my food. And it has spoiled me! Sometimes when I travel I'm not able to eat this way. I can taste the difference and I miss my real food.

Eating Like A Champ means choosing real food as much as possible. Crowd out processed foods by ignoring most food commercials and unregulated food labels claiming a product is healthy. I add in fresh produce and animal protein from local farmers when possible. When you must buy packaged foods, select toxin-free packaging, such as glass. Read food labels and select those with ingredients you recognize and limited to no additives, sugars and sodium. While some of these options may have more calories than some of the products you chose in the past, that is OK because not all calories are created equal. More calories from real food with healthy nutrients is more desirable compared to fewer calories from processed food; making this shift can help reduce cravings and even certain diseases.

4
EAT LIKE A CHAMP

THERE ARE LITERALLY HUNDREDS of dietary theories. This book doesn't focus on a specific program. Instead, I will discuss a few areas of nutrition that are relevant to consider as an Everyday Athlete: **1) Sugar, 2) Fruits and Veggies, 3) Protein, 4) Healthy Fats and 5) Water**.

Sugar

Did you know some medical professionals consider sugar to be addictive for some people? Do you have a sweet tooth? Do you crave sweets? You are not alone! Many Everyday Athletes will work out to compensate for their love of sweet treats. Candy bar + run does not equal wellness. It is OK to have a treat, but when you crave them frequently, it is a sign that you may have a sugar addiction. To break your sugar habit, you need to cut back on sugar. One simple way of crowding out sugar is to substitute water instead of pop and fruit drinks. Additionally, it is important to education yourself on the sources of your sugar as it might be hiding in a lot of the food you eat.

Perhaps you have made an effort to quit sweets without luck in the past. One reason may be because although you restrict obvious sources of sugar, you might still be feeding your sugar habit with other sources unknowingly. Many processed foods contain sugar and some may surprise you – fruit yogurts, cereal, spaghetti sauce, salad dressing, and juices. Items that are "fat-free" or "lite" often contain added sugar or sweeteners.

The American Heart Association recommends that men eat no more than 36 grams of sugar per day, and women no more than 20. 20 grams of sugar is equivalent to 5 teaspoons of sugar. To put this into perspective, one can of soda can have 40 grams, or 10 teaspoons, or sugar. Reading ingredients and labels is one mindful approach to monitoring your sugar intake. To combat the sneaky sugar in your food, you'll need to read labels. Look past the number of calories and confirm how much sugar the food contains. You'll be shocked by some of the foods that aren't a candy bar but are still full of sugar.

In addition to the amount of sugar on a label, review ingredients for added sweeteners. Often, you won't see "sugar" as an ingredient, but you might see high-fructose corn syrup. One of the easiest ways to spot sugar hiding in a list of ingredients is to look for words ending in the three letters "ose": sucrose, maltose, dextrose, fructose, glucose, galactose, lactose, high-fructose corn syrup, are all terms for sugar. The list doesn't stop there. Other synonyms for sugar include cane juice, dehydrated cane juice, cane juice solids, cane juice crystals, dextrin, maltodextrin, dextran, barley malt, beet sugar, corn syrup, corn syrup solids, caramel, buttered syrup, carob syrup, brown sugar, date sugar, malt syrup, diastase, diatastic malt, fruit juice concentrate, fruit juice crystals, golden syrup, turbinado, sorghum syrup, refiner's syrup, and ethyl maltol (Mottl).

As more Everyday Athletes begin Eating Like A Champ and are working hard to eat healthy, food companies are creatively adjusting their advertising. I've seen commercials for products boasting, "made with REAL sugar" or "100% organic sugarcane." Well, that is still sugar, even if it real and organic. Is organic sugarcane better than high-fructose corn syrup? I'd keep them in the same category and work to crowd them out.

Instead of your typical sugary treats, try including natural treats of real food like fruit of sweet vegetables including peas, carrots, sweet potatoes, or beets. There are many natural ways to add sweetness without the sugar. You can use local raw honey, 100% maple syrup, molasses, coconut palm sugar and stevia. These all can be used in cooking and baking as sugar substitutes.

My favorite treat is high-quality dark chocolate. If you like chocolate, and really what Everyday Athlete doesn't, pick a dark chocolate with over 70% cocoa to enjoy the full health benefits. It will be more expensive than your typical candy bar, but by spending a little extra to get the highest quality and peak health benefits, it is worth it. This dessert has a decent amount of fiber (4 times the amount in milk chocolate), is loaded with minerals, is a powerful source of anti-oxidants and has lower levels of sugar (about 50% less than milk chocolate) (Gunnars). I will enjoy a square or 2 from a Dark Chocolate bar once a day; it is A-OK to have treats in moderation when you are Eating Like A Champ! As you begin to crowd out sugar, you will be amazed to see your cravings for sweets subside. You'll also start to notice that certain foods are too sweet to enjoy. I remember when I first switched to plain Greek yogurt, I didn't care for the taste, but now when I taste the low-fat fruit on the bottom yogurt I used to have (which is full of sugar), I can't even eat it. Your taste buds will adjust as you detox from sugar and you'll enjoy real food so much more.

Fruits and Veggies

When you were a kid, did your parents tell you to finish eating your [enter whatever fruit or vegetable was on your dinner plate here] so you can grow up to be big and strong? Do you say that to your kids today? Well, your parents were right then, and you are right now.

One of the best ways to crowd out the junk you've been eating is to add in more fresh fruits and vegetables, especially vegetables. As a general rule of thumb, an Every Day Athlete should have 5 servings a day, at minimum. More is better! Strive for a variety of veggies, both in color and preparation to reap all the benefits.

There are many reasons why you should make sure you eat plenty of fresh fruits and veggies. You will get about 10-20 times more fiber in your diet; this will help make you feel fuller faster and thus help you achieve and maintain a healthy body weight. Filling up on fresh fruits and veggies means you'll have less room for sweet treats filled with sugar; less added sugar means more natural energy. The nutrients found in fruits in vegetables, which cannot be replicated by supplements, reduce risk for heart disease, diabetes, bone loss, and some cancers.

You should have at least 5 servings of fruits and vegetables a day, but more is better. Stick with Real Food - fresh produce is best in my book, and frozen is acceptable too, especially in winter when it's harder to have access to fresh produce due to weather in many areas. I generally stay away from canned produce as it often has preservatives and additives so it can sit on a shelf for a very long time, and therefore canned veggies can have less nutritional value.

Also, beware of juice! Many juices in stores are loaded with sugar, especially fruit juice. A good tip-off is if the label reads Fruit Drink or indicates it is made with real fruit juice; that means the beverage in question contains extra ingredients beyond pure fruit juice. Find something that is 100% juice, but even 100% fruit juice has a lot of natural sugars. Green vegetable juice offers more nutritional benefits, but the longer it sits before you drink will impact the overall nutritional value; fresh green juice is better. Unless you are making your own juice at home, I would skip the juice and drink water.

Increasing the amount of fresh fruit and vegetables is fun and you can get really creative. Here are my some of my favorite tips for sneaking in more fruits and veggies into your day using a sample meal plan with over 10 servings of fruits and veggies:

- Breakfast: The first meal of the day is usually a meal without vegetables; think outside the box to include a vegetable everyday with breakfast. Smoothies are a great way to add a couple servings of produce and start you day in a nutritious way. A general recipe I use for my smoothies: 2 servings of fruit + 1 veggie serving, usually a handful of greens, for example spinach + 1 cup of liquid, perhaps unsweetened almond milk. If you are really active and want some extra energy, add in some protein, such as plain Greek yogurt.

- Lunch: Eat your greens and have a salad. 2 cups of greens + 2 servings of other veggies + maybe even 1 serving of fruit. Top with some protein, like grilled chicken and some healthy fat, like avocado. You can also use these same ingredients and put in a wrap or a pita.

- Dinner: The food processor is your friend. Chop up 1-2 servings of veggies and sneak them into whatever you are preparing – for example, chopped carrots and spinach can hide in your marinara sauce or chili. Chopped cauliflower can sneak into homemade mac-n-cheese. Chopped bell peppers and mushrooms blend well with salsa.

One of the most common questions I get asked when I'm coaching my clients is about the importance of organic produce. Specifically, do Everyday Athletes have to eat all organic produce? There are a few different considerations. First, organic produce is grown without pesticides, chemical additives, or genetic modification. Organic farming also helps the environment by reducing pollution, preserving water and soil quality. But organic produce is more expensive than conventionally grown food, and for those of us who need to stick to a grocery budget, it can be difficult to buy all organic, all the time. My bottom line: While organic is better than conventionally grown, any fresh fruits and vegetables are better than no fresh fruits and vegetables – it is OK if you can't buy all organic produce.

A great way to prioritize your produce purchases is to follow the guidelines by the Environment Working Group (EWG) (www.EWG.org). Each year, this non-biased, non-profit group publishes a list of "The Clean 15" and "The Dirty Dozen" which you can get by signing up from their email list. The Dirty Dozen lists the 12 fruits and vegetables with the highest levels of pesticide residue. To avoid extra exposure to chemicals, prioritize your grocery budget to buy organic items listed on the Dirty Dozen. The produce on the Clean 15 list has the lowest levels of pesticides. It can be very helpful to keep the EWG list with your grocery list. Use the Dirty Dozen list to pick the produce to buy organic and/or use the Clean 15 to know which items you can buy conventional when needed.

If you are looking to save money on your grocery bill, it can help to shop locally and seasonally as well. By shopping at your local farmers market, you will get better prices than at the grocery store since small farms don't have the same over-head costs as big chains, like Whole Foods. Even if the selection isn't 100% organic, the produce will be fresher and likely grown using more sustainable practices compared to giant "agri-business" farms. When produce is in season, you can purchase it for cheaper prices compared to the "off season" when it is transported from warmer climates. If you stock up seasonally, many fruits and veggies can be frozen and enjoyed year round.

Eating Like A Champ means eating a variety of fruits and vegetables, throughout the day and throughout the year. To get the best results, seek out a variety of produce and prepare it in various ways to find what you like best.

Protein

Protein can be a confusing and controversial topic in nutrition. Everyday Athletes are confused about how much protein they need to consume and what sources they should seek. High-protein diets, such as the Atkins Diet, have been marketed for weight loss, which is appealing to many Everyday Athletes. And let's face it – the idea of eating lots of bacon sounds great. Bacon might make everything better, and having some bacon once in a while is fine in my book, but I don't think it should be a staple of a diet.

I have found a more balanced and mindful approach appropriate when considering protein consumption. Generally speaking, Everyday Athletes should be consuming protein to make up about 10-35% of their diets and spread it out throughout the day, but this will vary based on bio-individuality. Guidelines from the CDC indicate women should have approximately 46 grams of protein a day while men should have 56 grams, but these amounts may need to increase if you are doing some intense training (CDC). 46 Grams of protein is equal to approximately 6 ounces of chicken breast, about 2 servings.

The decision to consume animal protein is a personal decision and is greatly impacted by bio-individuality, but there are health benefits associated with crowding out red meat using plant-based protein sources. A diet consisting of large quantities of red meat can lead to heart disease and certain cancers, according to the National Institutes of Health (NIH) (Wein). Many conventionally raised farm animals are given antibiotics, are fed undesirable food, and they are kept in very uncomfortable and unsanitary conditions. The quality of the food coming out of environments such as these is questionable, in my opinion, and thus I consider it to be undesirable for those wanting to Eat Like A Champ.

Instead of conventionally raised animals, consider more humanely raised animals. Better yet, there are also many plant-based protein sources that can become a staple in the meal planning of an Everyday Athlete, such as legumes, lentils, nuts and quinoa.

There are many ways to crowd out animal protein. My family observes "Meatless Mondays" and sticks to a vegetarian recipe to start our week. I also usually have vegetarian meals for lunch. When I go out to eat and can't get information about the source of animal proteins, I tend to opt for vegetarian dishes. While I have reduced my consumption of animal protein quite a bit, I found I don't feel my best on a strict vegan or vegetarian diet. After a 3-day vegan cleanse, I had dreams of steak. After a few weeks of following a vegetarian meal plan while training for a half marathon, I felt very lethargic. Clearly, my body was sending me messages!

I have learned to incorporate humanely sourced animal protein into my diet a few times a week. I am lucky to have access to local sources at our farmers markets. While it is more expensive, I'm eating less meat, making it easier to work within my grocery budget. I accept that my bio-individuality requirements involve animal protein at this time and this is likely the case for many other Everyday Athletes. By adding in more plant-based sources of protein into your diet, you can crowd out animal protein and find the appropriate amount you need, which can vary based on factors including time of year or training schedules.

Everyday Athletes are very concerned about protein since it is a key component in assisting with recovery. As many Everyday Athletes establish their fitness regimen, they begin to wonder if they should be consuming protein shakes to help with recovery after a tough workout. Unfortunately, this is an area where marketing tactics lead to more confusion than helpful nutrition information.

While selecting real food is always my preference, I do realize sometimes a protein shake can be a quick and convenient way to consume protein after a tough workout, especially when more substantial food might be inconvenient to prepare and to eat for some Everyday Athletes. When opting for a protein shake, be mindful and be sure to read ingredient labels to search out recognizable ingredients and avoid the ones with high levels of added sugars.

When Eating Like A Champ, take note of your personal protein requirements. Aim for different types of protein, particularly plant-based protein, spread throughout the day. During periods of peak training, adjust your protein intake as needed.

Healthy Fats

Low-fat and fat-free diets are very popular and targeted toward health-conscious people who want to lose or maintain their weight. For many years, I would eat fat-free food thinking I was selecting the healthier option. My pantry shelves were stacked with 100-calorie snack packs of fat-free snacks, and I thought I was on the right track. Many people who are trying to lose weight or be healthy will pick the low-fat or fat-free option with the best of intentions. But fat-free isn't necessarily the best option, especially for the Everyday Athlete.

There are bad fats and good fats. We need good fat. Good fats can help us feel full and satisfied. When I was snacking on fat-free yogurt, I was usually still hungry after eating. I had cravings for sweets and more snacks. By adding in more healthy fats, I was able to curb some cravings. According to the Institute of Medicine of the National Academies, 20 to 35 percent of your daily calories should come from healthy fats (National Research Council). To calculate your daily fat grams, multiply the number of calories you consume daily by 20-35 percent. The fat-free trend is more about advertising and selling more products to people willing to pay to try to lose or maintain weight. But in reality, much of the processing that is done to remove the fat, that is naturally present in certain food, can actually make it less healthy. Often, lower fat foods contain sugar or other artificial sweeteners for flavor. By not consuming a certain amount of healthy fats, our body isn't getting what it needs and we end up with cravings. This can lead to unhealthy eating. And when your body isn't feeling satisfied, you will likely not feel great.

The key is selecting healthy fats. Some of my favorite options include hummus, avocado and olive oil. I will have hummus and fresh veggies as a snack, or add fresh avocado slices on my salad for lunch. Instead of buying fat-free salad dressing, I make my own with olive oil and fresh herbs. I have even switched to regular yogurt instead of low-fat yogurt. These items taste better than a fat-free alternative, and I often end up eating less than I would have with the fat-free option. Overall, they help me feel much more satisfied and they reduce my urge to snack and overeat.

Many Everyday Athletes may have low-fat snacks in their fridge or on their shelves. When you want to start Eating Like A Champ, take the time for a "makeover" to replace your fat-free purchases with the regular items. Keep in mind the concept of real food when making your swaps. Swapping fat-free potato chips to regular potato chips is not what I'm suggesting. Instead, swapping whole milk or unsweetened almond milk for skim milk or butter for margarine are the kinds of changes I'm suggesting. You heard me – ditch the skim milk! In some ways it might not be intuitive since advertising has led us to believe all fats are bad. It may take some mindfulness to integrate this change into your grocery shopping routine.

This was a tough change for me initially since I was so used to the Standard American Diet (SAD) and the concept of counting calories. Healthy fats have more calories than their lower fat substitutes. The idea of possibly eating more calories worried me as first since part of my motivation as an Everyday Athlete is to maintain weight. So I started slowly. After some time, I started to realize that the new healthy fats I was consuming was helping me crowd out other less healthy options including crackers and cookies. My favorite healthy fats (avocado and hummus) went great with fresh veggies, so it helped me eat more of those as well.

I try to add a small amount of healthy fats to each meal or snack to help me feel satisfied and full. For breakfast, I will add almond butter to my smoothies. For lunch, I will use my homemade salad dressing with olive oil and some fresh avocado slices. For a snack, I will have hummus and veggies. For dinner, I will add a little more salad dressing on my dinner salad or I will use coconut oil to roast my veggies. A small amount of healthy fats go a long way and have helped improve my activity levels as an Everyday Athlete as well. As you begin to Eat Like A Champ, take note of your current "fat-free" foods and begin to consider the healthy fats you can have to crowd those out.

Water

Hydrating Like A Champ is just as important as Eating Like A Champ. In some ways more so, because there are so many conflicting messages about hydration targeted to Everyday Athletes. It can be very easy to consume empty calories due to poor beverage choices, as well as calorie free options that have negative impacts to your health.

One of the simplest changes you can make to Eat Like A Champ is to increase your water consumption. You should be drinking approximately half your body weight in fluid ounces. If you weigh 150 pounds, you should be drinking 75 ounces of water per day. This is a good starting point, but there are factors of bio-individuality that will impact your water goals. Age, weight, geography, season, and intensity of workouts – these things can all impact how much water you need. Start with the guidelines and begin to notice how you feel and adjust as needed.

How much water are you drinking today? Most people aren't drinking nearly as much as they should. There are many benefits to drinking more water, such as increasing your energy. Your brain is comprised mainly of water according to the US Geological Survey (USGS) (Perlman). Drinking more water can help you focus and concentrate better; you will be more alert and have more energy. Water also helps to promote clear skin as it flushes out toxins and moisturizes your skin, removing wrinkles and giving you a healthy glow. Water also helps with weight management. Since it contains zero calories and fills your stomach, you feel full without eating as much. Sometimes, mindless snacking is driven by thirst rather than hunger, so reach for a water bottle instead of a sugary treat. Headaches, hunger, and tiredness – these are all signs that you may be dehydrated. Instead of reaching for a cup of coffee or a bag of chips when you are feeling tired or craving a snack, try a big glass of water first and see how you feel.

When I first begin working with new clients, increasing water intake is #1 on the agenda. There are a few common responses I hear. First, many people don't appreciate the taste of plain water and that will be a barrier to drinking more. Sometimes this is due to the other food and beverage habits impacting taste buds. If you are used to drinking diet soda all the time, water will taste weird at first. In these instances I suggest sticking with it. By drinking more water, your body will actually flush out toxins that could be influencing your taste.

There are many water additives marketed to improve the taste of water. Stay away from those since they likely include sugar or artificial sweeteners, even if they boast zero calories on their nutrition labels. Instead, you can add a healthy flavor boost with real food sources like fresh fruits, veggie and herbs. A few tasty combinations to try: strawberry and basil, blueberry and mint, and cucumber and lemon.

Using frozen fruit instead of ice cubes is a fun way to incorporate natural flavors in a cold glass of water. You can prep your healthy water in advance by filling up a pitcher or big water bottle with your ingredients, such as lemon slices and cucumber.

If you are used to drinking soda, consider sparkling water. You will appreciate the bubbles and there are many sparkling waters flavored with a touch of fruit juice. Sparkling water and club soda with a lime is also a great option in place of a cocktail when you are at an event or party.

I am a big fan of lemon water and often recommend this to clients. In the summer, I enjoy a cold glass of ice water with lemon wedges. In the winter, I will snuggle up with a warm mug of lemon water. A serving of lemon water a day can help boost your immune system thanks to the high amounts of Vitamin C and Potassium naturally found in lemons. It also helps with digestion and flushes out toxins better than water on its own. A glass of lemon water first thing in the morning is a great beverage to crowd out a regular morning coffee habit. If you usually start your day with a cup of coffee, try having a glass of water or a mug of warm lemon water instead, and waiting 20 minutes. If you still want coffee, have a cup. Before you help yourself to a second cup of coffee, try another glass of water. This same technique will also work with soda. Before you know it, you will be crowding out other beverages and drinking more water.

Another challenge that some people face as they try to drink more water is keeping track of how much water you drink. Many water bottles have markers that track the number of ounces along the side, so that can help you measure your water intake. Using mason jars as glasses can also work since they also have measurement information. Most standard sized glasses are about 12 ounces, so you can re-fill your glass several times a day as needed to meet your goal.

I fill up three water bottles a day and store in the fridge and work my way through them throughout the day. I know if I finish all three, I'll have had my fill. If lunch has passed and I'm still on my first bottle, I know I'm behind schedule. Sometimes I can feel myself losing concentration in the afternoons or developing a headache after a series of conference calls, and I'll know it's time to step away from my laptop and have a glass of water.

Many people will ask if coffee, tea or juice counts toward their hydration goals. I keep it simple and track only water. Drinking 8 cups of coffee is not the same as drinking 8 cups of water, and in many cases water can be used to crowd out other beverages with empty calories or negative side effects. Herbal tea is mostly water and is considered a healthy beverage, but I would still consider that something extra in addition to my pure water consumption.

It can be easier to drink more water in warmer weather. Cold ice water helps regulate body temperature and you may find yourself with increased thirst in a warmer environment. While your hydration needs might be reduced in the winter, you still need to stay hydrated. In fact, it can be more common to become dehydrated in cooler temperatures. Using hot or warm water (with or without lemon) can help, or even keeping your water at room temperature might be preferred during certain times of year. I've found it helpful to include certain spices in warm water in the fall and winter, such as cinnamon or turmeric. Spices have many of their own unique health benefits and add a natural flavor boost through leveraging real food.

As you begin to Hydrate Like A Champ, you may notice you are visiting the facilities more frequently. In most cases, this is a good thing since your body is doing what it's supposed to be doing by cleansing out toxins. Your body will adjust to proper hydration and the benefits of drinking more water will hopefully outweigh an extra trip to the bathroom or two. However, if you begin to notice a negative impact to your sleep, adjust your hydration habits so that you drink more in the mornings, and stop drinking water an hour or two before going to sleep.

Finally, be aware of water quality. Determine your local water quality by looking up a recent report. The Environmental Protection Agency's website, is a good resource to find details for each state. Water quality is determined by various factors, including harmful bacteria, lead from old plumbing, or even sand. If your research proves tap water may be unsafe, there are many types of water filters you can use to improve the quality of the water you are drinking. Bottled water is also an option.

By drinking more water, you will naturally crowd out many non-value-added drinks, such as soda and energy drinks. A 20-ounce bottle of soda has 16 teaspoons of sugar – would you want to eat 16 teaspoons of sugar on its own? Most likely not! The average American drinks 42 gallons of sugary drinks a year, which is the same as 39 pounds of sugar (Babey et al). Soda is one of the top items and Everyday Athlete should seek to crowd out of their daily nutrition plan.

Sports drinks are marketed to athletes, but much of the hype is just that – hype. Many sports drinks include added sugar and artificial sweeteners, which is not a healthy way to fuel your workouts. In some cases, an electrolyte drink would be beneficial, during or after a very intense workout, so choose wisely. Coconut water is becoming a more accessible option that is more natural and would be worth your consideration. Coconut water is naturally low in sugar and sodium and very high in potassium. Potassium can help prevent muscle cramping, so coconut water is an excellent choice for a post workout beverage or as the liquid base for a recovery smoothie.

To Hydrate Like A Champ Use, use water to crowd out sugary beverages. It is important to stay hydrated to feel your best as an Everyday Athlete. Bottom line – drink more water and less of everything else.

5
THE NUTRITION GAME PLAN

We have confirmed the link between food and fitness. We have reviewed some core nutrition concepts, topics and tips to Eat and Hydrate Like A Champ. Next, let's work through how to take action and build healthy habits through **1) Planning, 2) Accountability, 3) Tracking, and 4) Measuring Success**.

Planning

Fitness and food go hand-in-hand. How can the Everyday Athlete manage both when we already have so much going on? Planning is critical. One of the first tips I share with people when they are starting a new fitness routine or training plan is to create a documented plan based on your goals and then schedule your workouts. Many Everyday Athletes create plans in order to make daily progress toward their fitness goals easier. The same concept should be applied to your nutrition.

Many Everyday Athletes grew up playing sports. By developing an exercise routine through after-school practices or games on the weekend, they learned the importance of sticking to a regular fitness routine. Many of us can carry that habit into adulthood or have worked to develop a regular schedule that works for us. Perhaps your routine involves hitting the gym three days a week before work, yoga classes in the evening, or long runs on the weekend. We often track workouts in a calendar or journal. If this isn't a something you do today, I highly recommend it. By writing it down, you are making a commitment to yourself. It also helps minimize the decisions you need to make on a daily basis, and even makes it easier to commit to a workout. These processes can be applied to meal planning as well. By sitting down about once a week and writing down your daily meal plan, you can grocery shop appropriately and even do some meal prep in advance so you have healthy ingredients easily accessible for snacking and cooking.

Start small by planning one meal a day for a week. It might be easiest to plan for breakfast or lunch if you typically manage those on your own schedule. Or if you tackle dinners, you can enlist help from family in planning and prep. Don't worry about being perfect and having all meals planned. If that seems overwhelming, start small and gradually expand. If you want to tackle a full week work of meals, go for it.

Another important factor is to establish a realistic plan. While we should always aim to Eat Like A Champ, sometimes it's just not possible. Sometimes due to circumstances beyond our control, we don't have access to our usual healthy snacks. Perhaps you are at an event or working late. While you can do your best to plan for these scenarios, packing and bringing your own meals sometimes just doesn't happen. Do your best to make good choices with what is available and give yourself permission to be forgiven if you don't follow your plan perfectly. People often stray form their plans because their program is too restrictive.

While cooking at home is the best option to manage your nutrition, it is also fun to go out to dinner. It's fun to socialize with friends and try new types of cuisines. You can still Eat Like A Champ and have fun dining out. In fact, I encourage it! I'll often incorporate meals out into my plan and adjust accordingly. For example, if I want to check out the new Argentinian steakhouse on a Saturday night with my husband, I'll plan to make a salad with extra green vegetables on Sunday. When you dine in, you can make healthy choices but still enjoy your experience in so many ways. Portland is famous for Happy Hours, with menus offering a lot of appetizers and small plates at discounted prices. My husband and I have fun trying new restaurants by going to happy hours and sharing a few small plates rather than ordering restaurant-portion meals. When we go to one of our favorite places and order dinner, I try to pick something with veggies or I order a side salad. I'll plan to cut my portion in half and bring home leftovers. If we decide to have a dessert, we will often share it.

The key is to create a plan that is 80 percent healthy and 20 percent fun (within reason). You can have ice cream, but not a full pint of Ben and Jerry's every night. Allowing yourself some small splurges will help you enjoy your food and help you value the food you are using as fuel. Make good choices most of the time and don't beat yourself up if you veer from your plan. Many people establish strict plans that generate cravings and then they give into the cravings. By allowing a more balanced plan and some self-forgiveness, you are more likely to create a sustainable plan that you can incorporate into your life and benefit from the positive impact. Even if you start with small changes, your will see changes take place over time.

Pick a process to capture your plan that will work for you. It doesn't need to be complicated. A calendar to hang on your wall will work, as will writing down notes in a notebook. If you prefer to go paperless, there are many apps and gadgets that will work. Ask your friends and family if they have suggestions or read health and fitness magazines for tips. Bio-individuality plays a role in you how you will go about your schedule and planning. I use Google calendar so I can access my meal plan from my computer or mobile devices easily. I create a weekly plan for dinners and workouts and then develop my grocery list so I can shop on Sundays. When I was initially starting to Eat Like A Champ, I used a food and fitness journal for tracking, which we will review soon. There can be a little more effort up front establishing your planning process and finding a groove, but once you find it, you will have developed a healthy habit that is sustainable for a long time and it will help you Eat Like A Champ regularly.

Once you have your nutrition plan drafted, you can think though the prep work you can do in advance. For example, you can chop a variety of veggies and store them in containers so you will have easy access during the week for snacking and cooking. Another way to prep for the week is to make a big pot of soup that you can eat for lunches or even freeze for a quick meal later. I also will to wash and chop fruit and store in sandwich bags in the freezer so they are easy to grab in the morning to make smoothies when I need to make a quick breakfast. Certain nights of the week have a consistent theme in our house: Meatless Mondays, Pizza Fridays. I also keep my breakfasts and lunches very consistent; for example, in the summer I will sip a smoothie for breakfast and indulge with a colorful salad for lunch. This helps me fill in the blanks of my weekly nutrition plan quickly.

I know there will be nights when I'm too busy to cook, or I just want to sit and relax after a workout. I'm lucky because my husband will usually jump in to help. But on the nights when we both want the night off, it's good to have a few healthy options. I have discovered a local business that delivers organic meals to my home. I use this option when I know I'll be too busy to cook, but want a healthy meal. I have favorite local restaurant with a tasty chicken and vegetable soup that can be ordered as takeout on occasion.

Sometimes getting started is the hardest part of planning. A Health Coach can help provide you with some guidance and support to get a clear focus on your health goals and develop a plan to help you reach your goals by developing healthy food and fitness habits. If you tried to create a plan in the past without luck or your current plan isn't working, consider enlisting the help of a Health Coach. I have worked with my clients to support them with many small changes to develop a nutrition plan that works over time. They are able to see improvement gradually and have adopted healthy habits without even realizing it in some cases.

Accountability

You've put some thought into goals and developed a plan. Now it's time to take action. But starting a new routine is hard! Breaking through old habits and developing new ones can take effort. Having a support system is important. Tell your friends and family about your plan to Eat Like A Champ. Putting your goals out there and inviting others to be a part of your journey will make you more likely to succeed. When you go it alone, it can be easier to slip a day, or a few days, or just give up, especially if no one else knows. By having an accountability partner or a team for support, you will push through most days and keep your new habits going.

There are many ways to enlist accountability support. You can start with friends and family. My husband and I talk about our weekly meal plans, and most days we will talk about what we had for lunch. My husband works in an area with lots of fast food restaurants and he has even developed a "no go" list of the top restaurants he won't go to lunch at since he knows he'd order something unhealthy.

Friends can also be a wonderful source of support. I share healthy recipes with my friends and appreciate when they send recipe my way. By swapping healthy recipes, we end up talking about our nutrition plans and getting new ideas and inspiration for cooking healthy dishes at home. Perhaps you don't have face-to-face access to someone who is excited about eating healthy. That can be difficult, but social media has many channels in which you can "virtually" connect with others who are working to eat healthy.

You can find contacts through Facebook groups, Pinterest boards, Instagram hashtags, and healthy lifestyle blogs.

Bio-individuality can really drive how you hold yourself accountable. For some Everyday Athletes, having a partner for support or an online chat group of like-minded people with similar goals works wonders. Others may need to make a monetary investment in themselves to feel motivated to really work toward making their new habits stick. For some, a $40 investment in a new cooking gadget to make smoothies will help them start the habit of adding more fruits and veggies in a quick breakfast. Others may need a more significant investment to take action. Think about a price point that would push you to take action if applicable.

There are significant benefits to hiring professional support when undertaking goals to transform your nutrition. Sometimes friends and family will let you off the hook too easily and they don't have the knowledge and expertise to support you when you have questions or hit a roadblock. Finding a nutrition resource can help you wade through the plethora of often-conflicting nutrition information. They can also provide more rigorous accountability. Different health professionals have different styles and different areas of expertise. Think about your style and how you want to work with someone.

Health Coaches can help you define goals and develop a plan, and they will hold you accountable to taking action and executing your plans. They are knowledgeable resources when you have questions and can assist you in enhancing and updating your plan to help you establish realistic activities. I help my clients make small changes that they can stick to and then work day-to-day to see what is producing results. We also review what might require adjustments. We continue until a new health habit is ingrained.

Don't be afraid to ask for help. Most people don't want to bother others, but if you have Everyday Athletes in your circle, they'd probably love to support you. Everyday Athletes appreciate teamwork and want to help others in accomplishing goals. Once you are Eating Like A Champ, you might later have an opportunity to assist a fellow Everyday Athlete and share your experience.

Many Everyday Athletes don't think twice about having a workout buddy. It can help ensure you get up early and go to the gym or can turn a boring long run into a more enjoyable experience that goes by more quickly. I know the thought of having accountability for my nutrition was a new concept for me, especially when my primary goal didn't involve losing weight. Weight management is a priority, but for Everyday Athletes, the right nutrition plan can help fuel your workouts, so your accountability check-in will be more focused on how you feel before, during and after your workouts. Hold yourself accountable to incorporate changes to your plan when you aren't seeing progress toward your goal. It may mean asking tough questions and reflecting on your nutrition plan, pinpointing areas for improvement. **Focus on crowding out: Did you have at least 5 serving of fruits and veggies? Did you drink enough water? How much protein or healthy fats did you consume? Where can you add in? What healthy habits can you push further? If you aren't able to ask these questions of yourself, find someone who can.**

Find your way of sharing your nutrition with others and be open to ideas for improvement. Holding yourself accountable can be the difference between successfully adopting healthy habits and falling back into old ones. Be honest with yourself about what you can tackle on your own and what you need help with. Some Everyday Athletes are able to manage their own plans without support, while others may need support at certain times of the year. For example, the holiday season might be one time of the year when extra accountability is needed. Training for a big event may require additional support. Don't be afraid or disappointed in yourself if you need to ask for help; even elite athletes require a lot of support. While Everyday Athletes might not have access to the same types of resources as elite athletes, there are creative ways to find the right level of accountability and support. By remaining mindful of your nutrition and training plans, you will learn when and what types of support work best. Don't be afraid to try a few different techniques to find the ones that work best for you. If you check in with yourself and your intentions on a regular basis, you can be honest about what you need and when. Eating Like A Champ can require some assistance, but once you are **FEELING** like a Champ, it **WILL** become second nature.

Tracking

Now you have a plan. You have an accountability system. It's time for action! In order to develop your bio-individualized plan, it will be important to track your results and progress against your plan.

The tracking component to Eating Like A Champ will shed light on what works well and what will need to be adjusted. To help streamline your efforts, you can combine your tracking with your planning tools. Using your plan, indicate when you meet the plan and when you do not, and note the specific variances. Before drafting your next plan, review your variances and adjust as needed. Consider when your variances are driven by restrictions or cravings, and build in an appropriate change to ensure a realistic plan that you can sustain. Think about areas you can focus on to crowd out. It might take some time and effort initially as you begin to track, but know it will be worth it and the effort will decrease as you identify your personalized plan.

Many nutrition plans emphasize calorie counting as a primary mechanism for managing weight loss. I honestly have very mixed feelings on this. While calorie counting can be helpful to gain an understanding of portion control and how to quantify the fuel you consume compared to the energy you expend, I believe it misses some of the core nutrition concepts discussed previously. Simply counting calories will not give you the insight into the real food you consume. It doesn't indicate how much added sugar you are consuming. Counting calories won't inform you about nutrient consumption that comes with lots of vegetables and fruit. In many cases, when counting calories, a meal plan may lack the appropriate balance between proteins and healthy fats. In other words, counting calories will give you insight to quantity, but not quality. For this reason, I prefer to focus on Real Food and other Eat Like A Champ concepts: Lots of veggies, fruits and proper hydration. **Counting calories alone will not shed light into nutrient content or hydration levels for an Everyday Athlete.**

Using a nutrition journal is a helpful way to gather data and information so you begin to craft your bio-individual Eat Like A Champ nutrition plan. I also find it to be a helpful tool to leverage when I find myself straying from good nutrition. At the end of this book, you will find a helpful template to create a journal for your food and fitness plan.

When I track, I include both food and fitness components as well as water consumption and overall energy level. By having a consistent record of these data points, I can identify what works well and what does not. It also helps me find the best options for fueling tough workouts and promoting recovery.

Daily tracking may seem like a lot of work. Developing a streamlined approach with tools you find easy to use will help. Keeping detailed records of everything you eat might not be realistic for you. But know that the more data you have, the quicker your individual plan will be revealed and the detailed tracking can be scaled back.

Keeping a visual record can also be helpful and fun! Commit to taking photos of your meals for 1-4 weeks. Taking a quick picture with your smart phone is quicker than writing everything down. You can keep the photos to yourself for tracking purposes or you can share through social media for support.

Sometimes tracking may reveal habits of which you are not proud. Be honest with your tracking and work to create realistic plans to address bad habits. A Health Coach can provide support during this process if you find it difficult to tackle on your own. Be honest with your tracking, even if you don't like what you see. Accurate data will help you make appropriate changes and develop sustainable, healthy habits.

Even as a Health Coach, I will track my nutrition from time to time. It can be a helpful reminder to me to drink more water or eat more vegetables. It also helps me identify when I need to make changes. For example, I find that I make changes to my meal plans based on the season or based on my workout routine. I need to eat differently in summer versus winter or if I'm training for a half marathon versus doing 30 days of PiYo™, a fun workout that combines Pilates, Yoga and some cardio elements. Everyday Athletes will often mix up their workout plans, methods, frequency or intensity. It makes sense that we need to adjust our nutrition accordingly, and by tracking and journaling we can make changes as needed or enlist an expert, such as a trainer or Health Coach, for some help.

The journaling exercise can be done at the start and/or end of each day and reviewed holistically on a weekly and monthly basis. This practice will support your mindfulness efforts and help you develop awareness to your own bio-individuality.

Having this data can help you identify patterns. Perhaps there are days of the week or times of the month when your energy is lacking or you have certain cravings. Perhaps you Eat Like A Champ Monday through Friday but tend to slip up on weekends. You may already know about these patterns. Often having the written documentation to reveal certain patterns can provide the motivation you need to develop goals and action steps to break bad habits and develop new ones.

Many Everyday Athletes want to know what to eat before, during and after tough workouts. Tracking will provide valuable insights to confirm what you should and should not eat for these occasions. Recording these data over time will lead to a solid nutrition plan that you can rely on, and you will start to reap the benefits as seen in improved fitness results.

Measuring Success

Once you begin to establish a tracking methodology, you will also want to consider how you will measures success. Too often we measure success by a number on a scale. While weight management is important, there are also many other factors to consider when Eating Like A Champ. As an Everyday Athlete you are changing your body, transforming it into muscle. Since muscle weighs more than fat, you might be making real strides, but you may not see that on the scale when the numbers don't move very much. **Consider how your clothes fit. Consider your energy level. Consider your quality of sleep.** During some of my most successful moments, my weight never changed, but I decreased a pant size and was able to exceed my weekly running mileage targets.

As you begin to Eat Like A Champ, these metrics may better measure your success and quite possibly weight loss will be a benefit as well. But even if the number on the scale doesn't move much, wouldn't it be fantastic to have improved sleep at night and more energy during the day as your skinny jeans fit great? Also, your workouts will benefit as well as you have more energy.

As you are eating all this wonderful real food with more nutrients, you will also begin to experience broader wellness impacts. Nutrient dense foods have a variety of benefits including prevention of diseases and strengthening your immune system. While there is no guarantee that you will never get sick again, you might notice your colds are less frequent and you can push through it more quickly.

As you define your goals and how you will measure success, be sure to think about how you will reward your success. Bio-individuality will define how you create your reward system. Some people are motivated by a big reward at the end of a big project. Others will to celebrate the small wins. Recognizing progress as you take your journey to Eat Like A Champ will help keep you focused on sticking to your plan, especially when you are feeling frustrated. Rewards for small wins will also help prevent you from jumping off your wellness path during times of stress. When possible, do try to avoid establishing food-based rewards since that can be counterproductive to the healthy habits you are working to sustain. Instead, consider self-care activities, such as a massage or pedicure, or perhaps some new fitness gear or clothing. This way your celebration won't detract from your current success, but it will help setup you up for future success.

6
THE EAT LIKE A CHAMP PLAYBOOK

As a quick reference, here are the key concepts related to basic healthy eating habits for Everyday Athletes:

Mindfulness:
1. Pause for a moment before eating, and take 3 deep breaths.
2. Chew your food thoroughly, at least 30 times per bite.
3. Pause mid-way through your meal and consider if you are still hungry; it is OK not to be part of the "Clean Plate Club" when you are Eating Like A Champ if you are full.

Bio-Individuality
1. The nutrition plan (or fitness plan) that works for you might not work for someone else.
2. Take the elements of multiple dietary theories that resonate with you most to create your own unique nutrition plan.
3. Don't get frustrated when someone else's "perfect diet" does not work for you.

Crowding Out

1. Focus on healthy food that you want to add into your diet.

2. Don't focus on the food that you aren't allowed to eat.

3. Make gradual changes to your nutrition plan so you won't feel deprived or unsatisfied and you will build healthy habits.

Real Food

1. Eat more fresh, natural foods and less processed foods that come in a box.

2. Don't believe everything you see about food on TV or on packaging; just because something is marketed as healthy doesn't mean it is.

3. Buy more food from local farmers, and less from big food businesses.

Fruits & Veggies

1. Fresh fruits and veggies are best! Frozen is OK.

2. Organic is better. If you are on a budget, prioritize to buy organic food for the items listed on the EWG's "Dirty Dozen" if possible, but any fresh fruits and veggies are better than none.

3. Eat at least 5 servings of fruits and veggies a day, with more veggies than fruit, to Eat Like A Champ.

Sugar

1. Read food labels beyond the calories and review the amount of sugar per serving.

2. Check ingredients for sugar in various forms, like high-fructose corn syrup.

3. To add sweetness, use natural ingredients like pure maple syrup or stevia, and for a treat enjoy high-quality dark chocolate (70% cocoa or higher).

Protein

1. Work to add more plant-based protein into your diet and crowd out animal protein; try including Meatless Mondays into your meal planning.

2. If you do eat animal protein (and that is OK) find high quality, humanely raised, local sources whenever possible.

3. If you do opt to introduce protein shakes into your nutrition plan, read ingredient labels and find one with quality real food ingredients with no added sugar.

Healthy Fats

1. Crowd out low-fat, fat-free and lite foods from your meal planning.

2. Include a small amount of healthy fats, such as avocado or olive oil, throughout the day to help you feel full and satisfied.

3. One easy way to include healthy fats (and more veggies) regularly is by making your own salad dressing and having a salad every day.

Water

1. Drink more water: Increase your water intake (gradually if needed) to drink half your body-weight in ounces.

2. Use water to crowd out other beverages with empty calories and negative health impacts, like soda.

3. Add natural flavors to your water to make it more appealing, like fresh herbs and fruit.

Planning
1. Be consistent; create your plan on a regular day or time.
2. Start small if needed and gradually take on more.
3. Have a healthy back-up plan in case you don't feel like cooking or if you go out to eat.

Accountability
1. Put your goals out there and ask for help.
2. Find an Accountability Partner to support you, either in person or online.
3. Make an investment in your health; hire a Health Coach.

Tracking
1. Reference your plan and note any variances so you can make adjustments if needed.
2. Use a tool that works for you: a notebook, a calendar, an app.
3. Make notes about your energy levels and workout results to help you find your personalized Eat Like A Champ nutrition plan.

Measuring Success
1. Define how you will measure your success with a metric other than weight loss if possible.
2. Celebrate your success, both big and small, with rewards.
3. Pick rewards that aren't food-based to set yourself up for future success.

RECIPES

Are you ready to Eat Like A Champ? To help you, I've included a few of my favorite recipes that I include in my regular meal planning. I often share new recipes and menu plans with my clients. To find more recipes or information about my Eat Like A Champ Workshops and Meal Plans, visit www.ReniHealthCoach.com.

Breakfast

You need fuel to start your day, not just coffee. If you are short on time in the mornings, consider a smoothie or baked eggs that can be made ahead of time. For those of you who work out in the mornings, determine your specific bio-individual requirements regarding how much to eat before and/or after your workout. Some Everyday Athletes do great on an empty stomach, and some will need something light, like a banana or a smoothie. Your morning fuel intake also may vary based on the type and intensity of your workout.

Baked Eggs with Veggies and Goat Cheese - 4 Servings

Ingredients:

- 12 eggs
- 1 yellow onion – chopped
- 1 red bell pepper – chopped
- 1-2 cups mushroom – sliced
- 2 cups kale – torn into bite size pieces
- ¼ cup goat cheese crumbles
- 2 tbsp. extra virgin olive oil, divided
- Salt and Pepper – to taste

Directions:

1. Pre-heat oven to 350 degrees
2. Wash and chop all veggies
3. Sauté the sliced mushrooms over medium high heat until browned with 1 tbsp. olive oil; when done, set aside in a bowl
4. In that same pan, sauté the onions with 1 tbsp. olive oil over medium heat, when they start to soften, add the red peppers and cook a few minutes longer
5. Place the onion and pepper mix at the bottom of a glass baking dish (9 x 12) then add the mushrooms on top
6. Place the raw kale on top of the sautéed veggie mix

7. Whisk the eggs in a large bowl with a dash of salt and pepper

8. Pour the eggs evenly over the top of the veggies

9. Sprinkle the goat cheese on top

10. Bake the dish at 350 degrees for about 30 minutes, until eggs are cooked through (test with a fork or knife – insert into the eggs dish and there should be no runny, raw eggs)

11. Slice into squares, serve - I like to add hot sauce

12. Refrigerate any leftovers and have for breakfast the next day – this tastes good warm or cold

Banana Oatmeal Breakfast Bites – 8 servings (2 Bites per serving)

Ingredients:

- 2 bananas
- 1 cup whole rolled oats
- ¼ cup dried cranberries
- ¼ cup chopped walnuts

Directions:

1. Heat oven to 350 degrees
2. Mash the bananas
3. Combine mashed bananas and oats in a bowl
4. Add in cranberries and walnuts and mix well
5. Scoop out a tablespoon of the mixture and place on cookie sheet; repeat until all the mixture is used
6. Cook for 15 minutes
7. Let the bites cool and enjoy!

Blueberry Smoothie with Banana and Almond Butter – 1 serving

Ingredients:

- 1 serving Shakeology® or your Eat Like A Champ approved protein powder or ½ cup Greek yogurt
- 8-16 oz. water - can substitute 4 oz. water with 4 oz. of unsweetened almond milk
- 1 banana, sliced - Slice and freeze the banana the night before to give your smoothie a thicker texture
- ½ cup of fresh or frozen blueberries
- 1 tbsp. almond butter, with no added sugar
- Ice cubes - optional

Directions:

1. Mix all ingredients in blender and blend until smooth

Fruit and Yogurt – 1 serving

Ingredients:

- 6 oz. Greek yogurt
- ½ cup strawberries, sliced
- ¼ cup almonds

Directions:

1. Top Greek yogurt with strawberries and almonds and enjoy!

Pumpkin Oatmeal – 1 serving

Ingredients:

- ½ cup whole rolled oats
- 2 tbsp. pumpkin
- 1 tsp. cinnamon
- 1 tbsp. almonds
- 1 tbsp. dried cranberries

Directions:

1. Measure oats, pumpkin and cinnamon into a bowl
2. Add about ¾-1 cup of water
3. Microwave on high for 1 minute until water is absorbed
4. Stir all ingredients together and top with almonds and dried cranberries

Pumpkin Spice Smoothie – 1 serving

Ingredients:

- 2 tbsp. canned pumpkin
- 1 cup unsweetened almond milk
- 1 banana - Slice and freeze the banana the night before to give your smoothie a thicker texture
- ½ cup Greek yogurt
- 2 tsp. cinnamon
- 1 tsp. nutmeg
- 1-2 tsp. sunflower seeds – optional
- Ice cubes - optional

Directions:

1. Slice bananas, scoop the pumpkin and yogurt and add the spices
2. Pour almond milk over the mixture
3. Add in a couple of ice cubes – optional
4. Blend until smooth
5. Pour into glass
6. Top with an extra shake of cinnamon and a sprinkle of sunflower seeds – optional

Strawberry & Spinach Smoothie – 1 serving

Ingredients:

- 1 serving Shakeology® or your Eat Like A Champ approved protein powder or ½ cup Greek yogurt
- ½ cup of strawberries
- 1 cup baby spinach
- 8-16 oz. water - can substitute 4 oz. water with 4 oz. of unsweetened almond milk
- Ice cubes - optional

Directions:

1. Mix all ingredients in blender with ice and blend until smooth

Lunch

I like to incorporate leftovers from dinner into my lunches or items that I can prep ahead of time. That way when I'm busy with meetings and conference calls, I know I have a healthy meal ready and waiting for me when the time comes. It can be helpful to prep a big batch of food, like soup, over the weekend and divide it up during the week for lunches.

Garbanzo Bean Salad – 2 servings

Ingredients:

- 2-3 cups mixed greens
- 2 carrot, shredded
- 10 grape or cherry tomatoes, cut in half
- 2 tbsp. extra virgin olive oil
- 1 lemon, juiced
- 1 cup garbanzo beans, drained
- ¼ red onion, medium, diced
- 4 teaspoons sunflower seeds

Directions:

1. Whisk olive oil and lemon juice in a small bowl, place greens in a large bowl, drizzle with dressing
2. Add tomatoes, garbanzo beans, onion, and carrot on top of greens and sprinkle sunflower seeds on top

Quinoa Veggie Bowl – 1 serving

Ingredients:

- 1 serving leftover Simple Quinoa (see dinner recipes)
- 1 serving leftover Roasted Broccoli (see dinner recipes)
- 1 serving leftover Roasted Sweet Potato (see dinner recipes)

Directions:

1. Using your leftovers from dinner and mix together the quinoa, broccoli and sweet potato in a bowl
2. Microwave for 1-2 minutes on high or reheat in oven at 350 degrees for about 15-20 minutes

Roasted Butternut Squash Soup – 4 servings

Ingredients:

- 1 large butternut squash
- 4 cups chicken broth – low sodium

Directions:

1. Heat oven to 350 degrees
2. Pierce the squash with a knife several times
3. Place the squash in the baking dish, pour enough water to cover the bottom of the baking dish so the squash won't burn / stick to the bottom
4. Roast the squash for 45-60 minutes, rotating it several times during the process – it will be done when you can very easily slice it in the middle with a knife
5. When the squash is done roasting, pull it out of the oven and let it cool for a bit, until it is cool enough to handle with your bare hands
6. Slice the squash into quarters, scoop out the seeds and any stringy pieces and throw away
7. Then use the knife to peer away the skin – when skin is removed, chop the squash into cubes about 1 inch by 1 inch
8. Place the squash cubes into the slow cooker and turn it on low

9. Pour chicken broth over the squash cubes, filling it up enough so that all the squash is covered

10. Put the cover on the slow cooker and let it cook for 4-6 hours on low

11. Prior to serving, liquefy the squash using the handheld blender in the crock pot (or ladle out batches and use a food processor or regular blender – or use a hand masher)

12. Ladle out the soup into serving bowls and enjoy!

Variations:

- If you like a creamy soup, stir in ½-1 cup of milk just prior to serving

- Topping with a spoonful of goat cheese crumbles and/or fresh parsley adds excellent flavor

- I also like adding hot sauce – the spicy hot sauce and sweet butternut squash go great together

- If you don't have broth (or not enough broth), water will work OK too; you could also swap vegetable broth instead of chicken broth for vegetarians

Tuna Salad with Spinach - 2 servings

Ingredients:

- 3-4 cups of baby spinach
- 4 oz. water-packed tuna (drained)
- 10 cherry tomatoes, sliced in half
- 2 stalk chopped celery
- 5 green onions diced
- ¼ cup dried cranberries
- 1-2 tbsp. extra virgin olive oil
- 2-3 lemon wedges

Directions:

1. Mix together tuna, tomatoes, celery, onions, cranberries, and olive oil
2. Divide spinach into 2 bowls and place the tuna and veggies on top
3. Squeeze lemon wedges over salad for dressing

Veggie Avocado Wrap - 2 servings

Ingredients:

- 1 cup sliced white mushrooms
- 1 cup diced bell pepper
- ¼ cup diced red onion
- 1 avocado, mashed
- 2 cups mixed greens
- 2 large whole wheat tortillas
- 2 tbsp. extra virgin olive oil

Directions:

1. Sauté the mushrooms, bell pepper and onion with olive oil (tip: do this the night before!)
2. Spread the mashed avocado evening in the tortillas
3. Divide veggies across the 2 tortillas
4. Cover veggies with greens
5. Wrap up or eat with a fork

Veggie Hummus Wrap - 2 servings

Ingredients:

- 1 cup sliced zucchini
- 1 cup diced bell pepper
- ¼ cup diced red onion
- 4 tbsp. hummus
- 2 cup spinach
- 2 large whole wheat tortillas
- 1 tbsp. extra virgin olive oil

Directions:

1. Sauté zucchini, bell pepper and onion with olive oil (tip: do this the night before!)
2. Spread hummus in each tortilla, approx. 2 tbsp. in each
3. Place veggies in each tortilla
4. Cover veggies with spinach
5. Wrap up or eat with a fork

Snacks

Snacking is very dependent upon bio-individuality. Some Everyday Athletes do best with a mid-morning snack, some with an afternoon snack, and some will need both. More frequent, smaller meals can help regulate blood sugar and help prevent energy drops and mood swings. Snacking requirements may also vary depending upon your training plan. I feel it's better to be prepared than to feel suddenly crabby and craving a sweet treat late in the day. I like to keep some healthy snacks on hand just in case!

Carrot Chips and Avocado – 1 Serving

Ingredients:

- 2 carrots
- ½ avocado
- Salt and Pepper – to taste

Directions:

1. Slice carrots into "chips"
2. Mash avocado with a fork and season with salt and pepper to taste
3. Dip carrots into avocado and enjoy!

Celery and Almond Butter – 1 Serving

Ingredients:

- 3 celery stalks
- 2 tbsp. almond butter (with no sugar added)

Directions:

1. Spread almond butter evenly across celery sticks

Cucumber Slices and Hummus – 1 Serving

Ingredients:

- ½ cucumber
- 2 tbsp. hummus

Directions:

1. Slice cucumbers
2. Spread hummus evenly across all slices

Roasted Chickpeas – 4 servings

Ingredients:

- 1 12 oz. can of chickpeas
- 2 tbsp. extra virgin olive oil
- Salt - to taste
- Seasoning of choice

Directions:

1. Heat oven to 400 degrees
2. Drain and rinse chickpeas, blot dry with a paper towel
3. In a bowl, drizzle chickpeas with olive oil and season with salt
4. Season with other spices as desired
5. Spread evenly across a baking sheet
6. Bake for 30-40 minutes, until chickpeas are browned and crunchy
7. Watch carefully in final minutes so your snack won't burn

Trail Mix – 10 servings

Ingredients:

- 1 cup raw almonds
- 1 cup walnut halves
- 1 cup dried cherries
- ½ cup dark chocolate covered almonds
- ½ cup pumpkin seeds

Directions:

1. Mix all ingredients together
2. Scoop equally into 10 containers or zip lock bags for easy grab and go snacking

Dinner

By developing a few go-to meals that are easy to cook, you can help ensure you and your family is eating healthy dinners. To help increase your veggie consumption, it's a great idea to include a simple salad with dinner; there are a few different salads here you can choose from! I like to cook a little extra at dinner time and save for it for lunch the next day.

Apple & Goat Cheese Salad – 2 servings

Ingredients:

- 2-3 cups mixed greens
- 1 medium apple, sliced or diced
- 2 tbsp. crumbled goat cheese
- ¼ cup almonds
- 2 tbsp. extra virgin olive oil
- 2 tbsp. balsamic vinegar
- 1 tsp. Dijon mustard
- Salt and Pepper - to taste

Directions:

1. In a large bowl, mix vinegar, mustard, salt and pepper, whisk in olive oil and blend
2. Add greens to large bowl with dressing and toss well with dressing and divide into 2 salad bowls
3. Top with apple slices, goat cheese and almonds evenly

Autumn Quinoa Salad – 4 to 6 servings

Ingredients:

- 1 cup quinoa – cooked accordingly
- 1 large apple – chopped
- 1 large sweet potato – peeled and chopped
- 1 large bell pepper – chopped
- ¼ cup dried cranberries
- ¼ cup sunflower seeds
- 1 lemon – juiced
- 1-2 tbsp. extra virgin olive oil
- 1-2 tsp. chili powder - optional

Directions:

1. Set oven to 350 degrees
2. Spread peeled chopped sweet potato in baking dish, sprinkle in extra virgin olive oil and chili powder (optional) and mix together to ensure coverage
3. Roast sweet potato for 30-40 minutes, until cooked through
4. Prepare the quinoa and place in a large bowl
5. Add bell pepper, cranberries and sunflower seeds to the bowl and stir all ingredients together well
6. Add the diced apple to the bowl, pour lemon juice on top covering the apple well to help prevent the apples from turning brown, then stir again
7. When sweet potato is done, stir into the salad and enjoy! (Good cold or warm)

Baked Spaghetti Squash with Red Sauce – 4 to 6 servings

Ingredients:

- 1 spaghetti squash
- 1 28 oz. can of diced tomatoes (mostly drained)
- 1 14 oz. can of navy beans (drained)
- 1 large carrot
- 1 bell pepper
- 1 medium yellow onion
- 2 cloves of garlic
- 1 tsp. oregano
- 1-2 tbsp. extra virgin olive oil
- 2-4 fresh basil leaves – optional
- Salt and pepper – to taste

Directions:

1. Set oven to 350 degrees
2. Pierce the squash several times on all sides with a fork or knife
3. Place in baking dish with about 1/8 inch of water
4. Roast for 40-60 minutes, checking and turning every 15 minutes; it is done when you can easily slice a knife all the way through it
5. While your squash is roasting – make your red sauce

6. Chop the carrot, red pepper and onion into pieces small enough to fit into your food processor – throw it all in there along with your garlic and pulse until everything is easily chopped

7. Pour into sauté pan and heat on medium for about 5 minutes, seasoning with salt and pepper

8. Pour in diced tomatoes and oregano and keep on medium high heat until it starts to simmer, then turn to low

9. Pour in the navy beans and keep on low until squash is ready

10. Once squash is cooked and cooled enough for you to be able to handle it, slice off the end with the stem, then slice in half length-wise

11. Use a fork to gently pull out any seeds

12. Then, use a fork to scrape out the flesh of the squash – it should come out as strands and look like spaghetti noodles

13. Place the squash into a casserole dish and toss with olive oil, salt and pepper

14. Pour red sauce over squash

15. Sprinkle cheese evenly across the top

16. Bake for another 20-30 minutes until cheese is melted, garnish with fresh basil then enjoy!

Homemade Balsamic Vinaigrette Dressing - 10 servings

Ingredients:

- 10 tbsp. extra virgin olive oil
- 10 tbsp. balsamic vinegar
- 1 tsp. Dijon mustard
- Salt and Pepper – to taste

Directions:

1. Pour all the dressing ingredients into a glass jar and seal tightly
2. Shake until everything is mixed together evenly
3. Store in fridge; if ingredients separate / solidify while stored take out of fridge and let sit at room temperature for 30 minutes to an hour prior to serving; shake well before using

Honey Dijon Chicken – 2 servings

Ingredients:

- 2 chicken breasts
- ¼ cup Dijon mustard
- 1 tbsp. raw honey
- 1 tbsp. extra virgin olive oil
- ¼ cup fresh parsley, finely chopped
- Salt and pepper – to taste

Directions:

1. Mix Dijon mustard with honey, parsley, salt, and pepper
2. Coat the chicken breasts, both sides, with the marinade
3. Grill (or pan sear) for about 7 minutes on each side (or until fully cooked)

Kale and Avocado Salad – 2 servings

Ingredients:
- 3 cups kale – chopped
- 1 avocado
- ¼ cup red onion, chopped
- ¼ cup dried cranberries
- ¼ cup raw pumpkin seeds

Directions:
1. Dice the red onion and set aside
2. Measure out the pumpkin seeds and dried cranberries and set aside
3. Wash the kale in cold water
4. Tear the leafy part from the tough stems in bite size pieces
5. Spin dry in a salad spinner or pat dry with towel
6. Place in a large bowl
7. Slice the avocado in half, remove the pit, and scoop out the insides and place in the bowl with the kale
8. Squeeze the juice from the lemon over the avocado and kale
9. Using both hands, massage the lemon juice and avocado into the kale; the avocado should be spread to evenly coat all the kale
10. Add the onions, pumpkin seeds and cranberries and hand mix again
11. Divide the contents into 2 salad bowls for serving
12. Wash your hands, sprinkle a few extra pumpkin seeds on top to garnish and enjoy your salad!

Roasted Broccoli - 2 servings

Ingredients:

- 3 cups broccoli, cut into equal sizes
- 2 tbsp. Parmesan cheese, grated or shredded, your choice
- 1-2 cloves of garlic, diced
- 1-2 tbsp. extra virgin olive oil

Directions:

1. Set oven to 350 degrees
2. Place broccoli into over safe baking dish, drizzle with olive oil, garlic, salt and pepper
3. Roast until crisp/tender - about 15 minutes
4. Sprinkle with cheese while hot, serve and enjoy!

Roasted Sweet Potato – 2 servings

Ingredients:

- 1 large sweet potato or 2 medium, peeled and cut into equal sized cubes / bites
- 1 tbsp. chili powder (optional—if you don't like the heat, try cinnamon instead!)
- 2 tbsp. extra virgin olive oil

Directions:

1. Set oven to 350 degrees
2. Place sweet potato in oven-safe dish and coat with chili powder and olive oil
3. Roast Sweet potatoes - checking after 20 minutes, and stir so the potatoes don't stick to the pan - 30-40 minutes, until done

Simple Quinoa – 4 servings

Ingredients:

- 1 cup dry quinoa
- 2 cups water
- 1 tbsp. olive oil
- 1 tbsp. lemon juice

Directions:

1. Rinse quinoa in cold water
2. Add to pot with 2 cups of water and bring to a boil
3. Let simmer on medium / low for about 15 minutes, until water is absorbed
4. Remove from heat, add olive oil and lemon juice, fluff with a fork and let sit about 10 minutes

Simple Spinach & Tomato Salad – 2 servings

Ingredients:

- 2-3 cups baby spinach
- 10 grape or cherry tomatoes, cut in half
- 2-3 tbsp. homemade balsamic vinaigrette dressing

Directions:

1. Place spinach into 2 salad bowls
2. Spoon dressing equally and toss spinach for even coverage
3. Top with tomatoes in both bowls

Strawberry Spinach Salad with Chicken – 1 serving

Ingredients:

- 2 cups spinach
- 1 tbsp. crumbled goat cheese
- ½ avocado, sliced
- ½ cup cooked chicken, chopped
- 1 tbsp. raw almonds
- 1 cup strawberries, sliced
- 2 tbsp. homemade balsamic dressing

Directions:

1. Wash and place spinach into a big salad bowl
2. Spoon dressing over spinach and toss for even coverage
3. Slice strawberries and avocado and put on top spinach
4. Top with almonds and goat cheese
5. Add cooked chicken on top and serve

Summer Quinoa Salad with Chicken – 4 to 6 servings

Ingredients:

Dressing:

- 1 lemon, juiced
- 2 tbsp. extra virgin cold pressed olive oil
- Salt and Pepper – to taste

Salad:

- 1 cup dry quinoa, cooked accordingly
- 1-2 chicken breasts, cooked
- ¼ cup raw almonds
- ¾ cup each of red and yellow bell peppers, chopped
- ¾ cup blueberries
- 2 cups arugula, chopped

Directions:

1. Cook the quinoa – set aside and let cool
2. Prep the dressing in a large bowl – pour in lemon, olive oil, salt / pepper and whisk everything together
3. Chop the veggies, add to the bowl and mix with dressing until evenly coated
4. Gently stir in almonds, blueberries and quinoa
5. Top with cooked chicken
6. Refrigerate for at least one hour before serving and then enjoy!

Three-Bean Chili - 4 Servings

Ingredients:

- 1 large yellow onion
- 1-2 red bell peppers
- 1 14 oz. can of kidney beans, no/low sodium, drained
- 1 14 oz. can of black beans, no/low sodium, drained
- 1 14 oz. can of navy beans, no/low sodium, drained
- 1 28 oz. can of diced tomatoes, preferably San Marzano
- 1 tbsp. cumin
- 1 tbsp. chili powder
- ¼-½ cup chopped cilantro
- 4 green onions, chopped
- Salt and Pepper - to taste
- Optional: ½-1 pound of cooked lean ground turkey

Directions:

1. Chop onion and red pepper and place in crock pot
2. Season with cumin, chili powder, and salt and pepper
3. Open and drain three cans of beans and pour into crock pot – stir all ingredients
4. Open can of tomatoes and pour in crock pot – stir all ingredients again
5. Optional: Add turkey – stir all ingredients again
6. Cook on low for 4-6 hours
7. Top with cilantro and green onion, serve and enjoy!

Zucchini Cashew Soup – 2 servings

Ingredients:

- 35 raw cashews
- 3 cups of water, divided
- 3 medium zucchini, cut into chunks
- Fresh herbs like basil, dill and parsley

Directions:

1. Soak cashews in 1 cup of water for about an hour
2. While cashews soak, bring 2 cups of water to a boil
3. Add chopped zucchini to boiling water for about 5 minutes
4. Drain water from zucchini and set aside
5. Grab your fresh herbs and set them aside – a few basil leafs, a few stalks of dill, a handful of parsley
6. Once the cashews are done soaking, keep them with the water and combine with zucchini and herbs (set aside a couple of basil leaves)
7. Use an immersion blender or food processor to blend until smooth
8. The soup can be served warm or cold
9. If needed/desired, heat soup over medium heat (don't boil), for about 5 minutes, stirring frequently
10. Divide soup into 2 bowls, garnish with fresh basil (optional) and enjoy!

DAILY FOOD AND FITNESS JOURNAL

To HELP GET YOU started on your journey, here is a simple journal template you can use to plan and track your food and fitness. Once this is full, you can download additional pages from my website: www.ReniHealthCoach.com.

DAY 1

Date: _____

Goal: _____

_____

_____

Action items to support my goal:

✓ _____

✓ _____

✓ _____

	PLAN	ACTUAL
Workout		
Breakfast		
Lunch		
Dinner		
Snack		
Water		

Comments/Notes:

_____

_____

Energy Level:

1   2   3   4   5   6   7   8   9   10

DAY 2

Date: _____

Goal: _____

_____

_____

Action items to support my goal:
- ✓ _____
- ✓ _____
- ✓ _____

	PLAN	ACTUAL
Workout		
Breakfast		
Lunch		
Dinner		
Snack		
Water		

Comments/Notes:

_____

_____

Energy Level:

1   2   3   4   5   6   7   8   9   10

DAY 3

Date: _____

Goal: _____

_____

_____

Action items to support my goal:

✓ _____

✓ _____

✓ _____

	PLAN	ACTUAL
Workout		
Breakfast		
Lunch		
Dinner		
Snack		
Water		

Comments/Notes:

_____

_____

Energy Level:

1   2   3   4   5   6   7   8   9   10

DAY 4

Date: _____

Goal: _____
_____
_____
_____

Action items to support my goal:
- ✓ _____
- ✓ _____
- ✓ _____

	PLAN	ACTUAL
Workout		
Breakfast		
Lunch		
Dinner		
Snack		
Water		

Comments/Notes:
_____
_____

Energy Level:

1   2   3   4   5   6   7   8   9   10

DAY 5

Date: _____

Goal: _____

_____

_____

Action items to support my goal:

✓ _____

✓ _____

✓ _____

	PLAN	ACTUAL
Workout		
Breakfast		
Lunch		
Dinner		
Snack		
Water		

Comments/Notes:

_____

Energy Level:

1   2   3   4   5   6   7   8   9   10

DAY 6

Date: _____

Goal: _____

_____

_____

Action items to support my goal:

✓ _____

✓ _____

✓ _____

	PLAN	ACTUAL
Workout		
Breakfast		
Lunch		
Dinner		
Snack		
Water		

Comments/Notes:

_____

Energy Level:

1   2   3   4   5   6   7   8   9   10

DAY 7

Date: _____

Goal: _____
_____
_____

Action items to support my goal:
- ✓ _____
- ✓ _____
- ✓ _____

	PLAN	ACTUAL
Workout		
Breakfast		
Lunch		
Dinner		
Snack		
Water		

Comments/Notes:
_____

Energy Level:

1   2   3   4   5   6   7   8   9   10

DAY 8

Date: _____

Goal: _____
_____
_____
_____

Action items to support my goal:
- ✓ _____
- ✓ _____
- ✓ _____

	PLAN	ACTUAL
Workout		
Breakfast		
Lunch		
Dinner		
Snack		
Water		

Comments/Notes:
_____

Energy Level:

1   2   3   4   5   6   7   8   9   10

DAY 9

Date: _____

Goal: _____

_____

_____

Action items to support my goal:

✓ _____

✓ _____

✓ _____

	PLAN	ACTUAL
Workout		
Breakfast		
Lunch		
Dinner		
Snack		
Water		

Comments/Notes:

_____

_____

Energy Level:

1   2   3   4   5   6   7   8   9   10

DAY 10

Date: _____

Goal: _____

_____

_____

_____

Action items to support my goal:

✓ _____

✓ _____

✓ _____

	PLAN	ACTUAL
Workout		
Breakfast		
Lunch		
Dinner		
Snack		
Water		

Comments/Notes:

_____

Energy Level:

1   2   3   4   5   6   7   8   9   10

DAY 11

Date: _____

Goal: _____

_____

_____

Action items to support my goal:

✓ _____

✓ _____

✓ _____

	PLAN	ACTUAL
Workout		
Breakfast		
Lunch		
Dinner		
Snack		
Water		

Comments/Notes:

_____

_____

Energy Level:

1   2   3   4   5   6   7   8   9   10

DAY 12

Date: _____

Goal: _____

_____

_____

_____

Action items to support my goal:
- ✓ _____
- ✓ _____
- ✓ _____

	PLAN	ACTUAL
Workout		
Breakfast		
Lunch		
Dinner		
Snack		
Water		

Comments/Notes:

_____

_____

Energy Level:

1   2   3   4   5   6   7   8   9   10

DAY 13

Date: _____

Goal: _____

_____

_____

Action items to support my goal:

✓ _____

✓ _____

✓ _____

	PLAN	ACTUAL
Workout		
Breakfast		
Lunch		
Dinner		
Snack		
Water		

Comments/Notes:

_____

_____

Energy Level:

1   2   3   4   5   6   7   8   9   10

DAY 14

Date: _____

Goal: _____
_____
_____

Action items to support my goal:
- ✓ _____
- ✓ _____
- ✓ _____

	PLAN	ACTUAL
Workout		
Breakfast		
Lunch		
Dinner		
Snack		
Water		

Comments/Notes:
_____

Energy Level:

1   2   3   4   5   6   7   8   9   10

DAY 15

Date: _____

Goal: _____

_____

_____

Action items to support my goal:

✓ _____

✓ _____

✓ _____

	PLAN	ACTUAL
Workout		
Breakfast		
Lunch		
Dinner		
Snack		
Water		

Comments/Notes:

_____

_____

Energy Level:

1   2   3   4   5   6   7   8   9   10

DAY 16

Date: _____

Goal: _____

_____

_____

_____

Action items to support my goal:

✓ _____

✓ _____

✓ _____

	PLAN	ACTUAL
Workout		
Breakfast		
Lunch		
Dinner		
Snack		
Water		

Comments/Notes:

_____

Energy Level:

1   2   3   4   5   6   7   8   9   10

DAY 17

Date: _____

Goal: _____
_____
_____

Action items to support my goal:
- ✓ _____
- ✓ _____
- ✓ _____

	PLAN	ACTUAL
Workout		
Breakfast		
Lunch		
Dinner		
Snack		
Water		

Comments/Notes:
_____
_____

Energy Level:

1   2   3   4   5   6   7   8   9   10

Eat Like A Champ

DAY 18

Date: _____

Goal: _____
_____
_____
_____

Action items to support my goal:
- ✓ _____
- ✓ _____
- ✓ _____

	PLAN	ACTUAL
Workout		
Breakfast		
Lunch		
Dinner		
Snack		
Water		

Comments/Notes:
_____

Energy Level:

1   2   3   4   5   6   7   8   9   10

DAY 19

Date: _____

Goal: _____

_____

_____

Action items to support my goal:
- ✓ _____
- ✓ _____
- ✓ _____

	PLAN	ACTUAL
Workout		
Breakfast		
Lunch		
Dinner		
Snack		
Water		

Comments/Notes:

_____

_____

Energy Level:

1   2   3   4   5   6   7   8   9   10

DAY 20

Date: _____

Goal: _____
_____
_____

Action items to support my goal:
- ✓ _____
- ✓ _____
- ✓ _____

	PLAN	ACTUAL
Workout		
Breakfast		
Lunch		
Dinner		
Snack		
Water		

Comments/Notes:
_____

Energy Level:

1   2   3   4   5   6   7   8   9   10

DAY 21

Date: _____

Goal: _____

_____

_____

Action items to support my goal:

✓ _____

✓ _____

✓ _____

	PLAN	ACTUAL
Workout		
Breakfast		
Lunch		
Dinner		
Snack		
Water		

Comments/Notes:

_____

_____

Energy Level:

1   2   3   4   5   6   7   8   9   10

WORKS CITED

Babey SH, Jones M, Yu H, Goldstein H. Bubbling Over: Soda Consumption and Its Link to Obesity in California. UCLA Center for Health Policy Research and California Center for Public Health Advocacy, 2009.

"Crowding Out: The Healthy Way to Ride Out the Holidays." Institute for Integrative Nutrition. Institute for Integrative Nutrition, 17 Nov. 2014. Web. 02 Feb. 2015.

"Environmental Working Group." Environmental Working Group. N.p., n.d. Web. 02 Feb. 2015.

"Fast Facts - Soda and Sugary Drinks | Kick the Can | Physical Activity and Nutrition Policy Adoption in CA Cities." KickTheCan. California Center for Public Health Advocacy, n.d. Web. 01 Feb. 2015.

Gunnars, Kris. "7 Proven Health Benefits of Dark Chocolate (No. 5 Is Best)." Authority Nutrition. Authority Nutrition, 05 June 2013. Web. 02 Feb. 2015.

"How To Spot Sugar On Food Labels." Hungry For Change. Hungry for Change, n.d. Web. 02 Feb. 2015.

Krishan, Shubhra. "How Your Taste Buds Can Aid Weight Loss." How Your Taste Buds Can Aid Weight Loss. Care2, 10 Sept. 2013. Web. 02 Feb. 2015.

Mottl, Pooja R. "Food Labels: How to Spot Hidden Sugars." The Huffington Post. TheHuffingtonPost.com, 25 May 2011. Web. 04 Feb. 2015.

National Research Council. Dietary Reference Intakes for Energy, Carbohydrate, Fiber, Fat, Fatty Acids, Cholesterol, Protein, and Amino Acids (Macronutrients). Washington, DC: The National Academies Press, 2005.

Perlman, Howard. "The Water in You." Water Properties: (Water Science for Schools). US Department of the Interior - US Geological Survey, 17 Mar. 2014. Web. 31 Jan. 2015.

"Protein." Centers for Disease Control and Prevention. Centers for Disease Control and Prevention, 04 Oct. 2012. Web. 02 Feb. 2015.

Rosenthal, Joshua. Integrative Nutrition: Feed Your Hunger for Health and Happiness. New York, NY: Integrative Nutrition Pub., 2008. Print.

Rosenthal, Joshua. "Notes from IIN's Founder: Why It's OK to Quit Being Vegan or Macrobiotic." Institute for Integrative Nutrition. Institute for Integrative Nutrition, 3 Mar. 2013. Web. 02 Feb. 2015.

Wein, Harrison. "Risk in Red Meat? - National Institutes of Health (NIH)." U.S National Library of Medicine. U.S. National Library of Medicine, 26 Mar. 2012. Web. 02 Feb. 2015.

"What Is Macrobiotics?" What Is Macrobiotics. Kushi Institute, n.d. Web. 02 Feb. 2015.

Zeratsky, Katherine. "Nutrition and Healthy Eating." What Is BPA? Should I Be Worried about It? Mayo Clinic, 21 Mar. 2013. Web. 01 Feb. 2015.

ABOUT THE AUTHOR

Reni Towns lives in Portland, Oregon with her husband and two retired racing Greyhounds. She is a Project Management Professional (PMP) with over 15 years of corporate experience and is a Certified Health Coach. She is also an Everyday Athlete.

Reni grew up near Chicago, Illinois, playing basketball, soccer and volleyball. She went on to play and eventually serve as Captain for the Division 3 Women's Soccer Team at Lake Forest College in Lake Forest, Illinois. Fitness continues to play a role in her life. As an Everyday Athlete, she runs in several races a year: 5Ks, 10Ks and an occasional half marathon. She also enjoys PiYo™, yoga and strength training. In her Health Coaching practice, she partners with busy professionals to create energizing work-life flexibility through simple food and fitness habits. To learn more about Reni's health coaching programs, visit **www.ReniHealthCoach.com**.

Printed in Great Britain
by Amazon